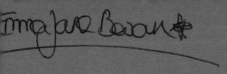

The
Business
of
Design

The
Business
of
Design

Ian Linton

Van Nostrand Reinhold (UK) Co. Ltd

First published in 1988 by
Van Nostrand Reinhold (UK) Co. Ltd
Molly Millars Lane, Wokingham, Berkshire, England

Typeset in 10/11 pt Sabon by
Best-set Typesetter Ltd., Hong Kong

Printed and bound in Great Britain by
T.J. Press (Padstow) Ltd., Padstow, Cornwall

British Library Cataloguing in Publication Data

Linton, Ian
   The business of design.
   1. Design – Management
   I. Title
   658'.0024741   NK1520

ISBN 0-7476-0007-4

Contents

Introduction

The Business of Design is a book for practising designers who find themselves responsible for managing a business. While much of their time will be
spent in designing for clients, an increasing amount of time will be spent in
project management and administration. Anyone who has been brought up
in the traditional art college system will have had little practical training in
this area and can only learn by experience. But already, there are designers
who have built up considerable experience in managing businesses employing 50 or more people, while at the top end of the business there are
design groups employing hundreds of people and run by professional
managers. Yet, it is not an unusual step for someone with responsibility for
a large consultancy to leave and set up a small practice.

Given the diversity of people who will be managing a design business,
what level should this book be pitched at? A primer on business management would be of little value to someone already running a consultancy,
while management principles might seem irrelevant to some of the problems
designers face. At the same time, to omit the basics of management would
leave the book without direction and without the basic information that a
beginner to management needs. So, the book is deliberately written at a dual
level.

Introductory text to each section describes the issues that designers face;
wherever possible, it is based on accounts of designers' actual experiences in
solving management problems, and it illustrates the varying ways in which
different designers have tackled the same problem. For the experienced
designer/manager, this section will give an account of contemporary
practice which may provide a stimulus to action. For the newcomer to
management, it provides a focus on the business of design, showing why
management principles are essential and how they help to deal with problems they are likely to face.

The second level of text is a structured reference section explaining the
basic principles of management that relate to those problems. It is a
foundation course, and we make no apologies for its simplicity. Because of
its structure – techniques and subjects – readers can dip into the section
whenever they need guidance on a specific point, or they can read it all the
way through as an introductory course.

At a more advanced level of business management, the need for professional advice and support increases; the reader who wants to know more is directed to additional sources of information and other services.

The book concentrates on the three factors that are essential to the success of a consultancy business – the management of time, control of finance and the management of people. The central portion of the book discusses the progress of a design project from identifying prospects through to relations with customers, while the final chapters concentrate on business management, showing how to use modern technology effectively and how to plan for expansion.

The Business of Design is written for the practising designer, not for the professional manager. Naturally this definition is going to cover a wide range of skills and experience, as well as a diversity of business situations. Management is just as important to the graduate who may be forced to work freelance, the freelance who has outgrown his own capacity, the designer who has been offered a partnership, or the senior partner who faces the challenge of expanding the business.

ONE
Business Matters

The business of design, or should it be the profession of design? The argument is bound to rage wherever good designers meet. Whatever the outcome of the argument, the fact remains that designers have to make a profit. No profit, no future. It's a simple and dramatic equation. Anyone who is trading as a designer has to meet costs out of the income that is earned. Yet, when the pressure is on to complete the work on the board, considerations of business naturally take second place.

In industry it is likely to be a different story. The person who makes the products is rarely the person who is running the company. Finance and accounting, sales and marketing, production planning and control are all specialist functions handled by full-time managers; the larger the company, the more formal the organization.

If you turn to the service industries, however, and, in particular, to the professions, the owners of the business are actively involved in providing the service. So where does that leave management? Simply being a good designer turns out to be insufficient. To quote the prospectus of the Design Enterprise Programme, 'Suddenly, you're a salesman, chief negotiator, senior buyer, book-keeper and financial controller. You're expected to deal with your bank manager, the tax man, the VAT man, the factory inspectorate, the local authority planners and suppliers.' While designers are producing superb creative work for their clients, they may not be enjoying the full reward for their efforts. In practical terms, this means asking questions like, 'How much should I charge for my work? How can I make sure that there is enough future work to generate cash when it is needed? Do I know really how well or how badly I'm doing?'

David Davies, head of design consultancy David Davies Associates, told Design and Art Direction, 'We are saying that design is a service which can help other people's businesses work better, and our own industry should reflect that. It should be run in a businesslike way.' Coley, Porter, Bell and Partners, a consultancy with its base in packaging design, believed that design's reluctance to become professional was one of the factors that inhibited its growth and its acceptance by industry. Too many designers, they felt, believed that professionalism was at odds with creativity.

It's not just the designers who think they ought to improve their performance. Design consultants, The Design Network, carried out a survey of two hundred design clients in 1985. Ninety per-cent of those who replied thought that design was a valuable marketing tool, but half thought that designers didn't appreciate their business objectives, and one-third of the respondents thought designers were more interested in satisfying their creative egos.

The problem is not confined to design, however. In 1985, *Campaign* magazine published an article called 'Victims of the Management Trap' in which they suggested that there were four main problems facing most types of consultancy (see also *Design Week* survey, pp. 9–10):

- They are bad at managing their own business.
- Clients are reluctant to pay designers at the same rates as other consultants.
- Consultants are unable to quantify the results and benefits of their work.
- They are bad at recruiting, training and retaining skilled staff in a business where people accounted for the highest percentage of assets.

How, you might ask, does all that help you win the next job? The immediate answer is that it does not. But, if you ignore the business of design, you may not be in a position to present for another job.

Michael Peters began his packaging consultancy in the 1960s. He had built an excellent client list, a profitable fee structure and a good workload. Then one bad debt nearly put the company out of business. As he admitted to *Design* magazine at the time, he didn't know enough about his business to pinpoint the trouble or set up a rescue operation (see Chapter 3, page 41). His response was to bring in a management consultant, Bob Silver, who very quickly introduced tight financial controls and helped him develop a plan for expansion. By 1983, the Michael Peters Group had become a public company on the Unlisted Securities Market. Michael Peters himself has a reputation in the industry as one of the most businesslike of designers, and the consultant, Bob Silver, remains deputy chairman of the group.

Success has brought the group a new management challenge. A public company is owned by a very large number of private and institutional shareholders, and the company's performance is under continuous scrutiny by City analysts. A drop in profits, a loss of business, or the departure of a key member of staff suggests a drop in performance, and this can bring the company's share price down and restrict its access to funds. As Michael Peters explained to *Direction* in 1986, the group's task was to grow at a rate fast enough to please the City, but not so fast that it transformed the quality of design. The group grew by diversifying away from packaging into new areas such as exhibitions, annual reports, product development, financial communications and marketing consultancy (see also Chapter 6, page 100). Good management was even more important, yet Peters admitted that he still thought of himself, first and foremost, as a designer.

Success does not always benefit a company. Fitch & Co, one of the largest UK design practices, found that the sheer size of the organization weighed against the ambitions of some of their top staff. Fitch gained a reputation as the 'charm school' of the design business and many ex-Fitch people are now running their own successful consultancies. In 1985, Rodney Fitch held a reunion party for Fitch breakaways, and his guest list read like a who's who of contemporary design.

Recognizing the problems that size can bring, Pentagram – who have enjoyed a reputation for design excellence since the early 1960s – have declared themselves firmly against any policy of growth for its own sake. Pentagram, in the minds of its founding partners, would never become a public company. At the same time they recognize the value of a businesslike attitude, and they have long been associated with Peter Gorb, a consultant in small business management. Peter Gorb explained in the Pentagram book, *Living By Design*, how he helped Pentagram develop a management structure that was right for five founding partners who were all active designers and leaders in their own specialist field (see also Chapter 4, page 68). It was an unobtrusive form of management that let the designers get on with their main task – producing good design.

Management problems are not confined to large consultancies. Eye of the Tiger was a small graphics group that had an extraordinary run of success in record sleeve design. The leading companies were throwing work at them, one of the partners recalled; he described the atmosphere as 'like world war three'. Suddenly, one major client pulled out and business 'went through the floor'. The group sold its way out of trouble, but it quickly diversified into other areas of design and vowed never to rely on one major client again. Not that it's always easy to change direction so quickly. Coley, Porter, Bell and Partners told *Graphics World* how they planned to become one of the top ten UK design consultancies by 1990. Their basic activity, packaging design, they felt would not give them sufficient growth to achieve that (see also Chapter 6, page 96). They needed to diversify, and they saw retail and corporate identity as the areas with greatest potential. Their problem was not a lack of ability in either discipline, but the reputation they had built up. Clients saw them as packaging specialists and could not make the mental leap to see them as designers on a broad canvas.

Sometimes, the management problem has little to do with design, yet its implications for a practice are considerable. The Jim Allen Design Team had outgrown its premises and planned a move that would give them room for expansion. A simple enough task at first sight, but it was a year and many traumatic experiences later that they finally moved in. On the way, they encountered local authorities who seemed unable to give design a classification, premises that revealed hidden flaws and landlords whose sole aim seemed to be tying their tenants' hands with legal clauses.

To the question, 'Does business management matter?', the answer must be yes, and the management skills take many forms. As the examples show, finance, marketing and personnel skills are essential – whatever the size of the consultancy – and there is no simple answer to the arguments over growth and expansion. There are two sides to management, however. Dealing with day-to-day problems is the negative side – management by necessity. But, on the positive side, there are tremendous opportunities for designers in the mid 1980s and effective management can help them to benefit from the opportunities. Design has never had a higher profile. BBC-2 broadcast Designs on Britain, the government appointed its first minister responsible for design, while the Prime Minister took part in Designs on

Britain and invited leaders of design, advertising and industry to Downing Street to launch the Better Made in Britain campaign. The public flagwaving exercise for design ran in parallel with the Design Council's Funded Consultancy Scheme which encouraged industry to try design without a heavy financial commitment.

These developments gave a great boost to product design, but the other sectors had plenty of attention. Channel 4's series on marketing explained the role that David Davies Associates played in developing the highly successful Next retail chain. The newly-appointed head of the Design Council – chief executive of WH Smith – recognized the importance of design in the retail sector by implementing a redesign of all his stores in 1986.

Packaging design enjoyed continuous growth throughout the 1980s, but Tesco gave it an unexpected bonus when it laid down a policy of high design standards and individual treatment for its extensive range of own-label products. Tesco didn't confine itself to a small group of design consultancies, but gave equal opportunity to large and small consultancies alike. The Big Bang in the City in 1986 revolutionized the way financial institutions carried out their business. Banks, building societies and stockbrokers found themselves in competition with each other. They were offering new services and there was a rash of mergers to take advantage of the new competitive opportunities. For the designers, it meant a boom in corporate identity and publications work (see also Chapter 2, page 32).

In such a heady atmosphere, it was not surprising that two new independent magazines for designers were launched. *Design and Art Direction*, published initially as a free supplement to *Campaign*, became a separate magazine in August 1986 and it was closely followed in September by the launch of *Design Week*, a stablemate to the highly successful *Creative Review*. Further indication of design's rise from cottage industry to mainstream marketing activity was demonstrated by the interest in consultancies shown by advertising agencies. Saatchi and Saatchi set up an independent design company within its global empire; several design consultancies formed more or less formal associations with advertising agencies; and one of the fastest growing communications groups – WPP, set up by former Saatchi financial director, Martin Sorrell – quickly moved into the top ten UK design consultancies, acquiring on the way three practices already in the top fifty in their own right. Design was now an established part of the marketing services business.

This led to moves within the design industry to strengthen the position of the consultancy. In 1985, delegates from most of the leading consultancies met to press for a new trade association that would give stronger representation of their interests. Their move was seen to be in conflict with the aims of the Society of Industrial Artists and Designers (SIAD) – now the Chartered Society of Designers – and threatened to split the movement. But a compromise was reached, and in 1986 the Design Business Group (DBG) was set up within SIAD to help consultancies make the most of the new business opportunities. Eight hundred design consultancies were invited to join DBG, which saw its major role as improving professional standards. With that in mind, it set up five subcommittees to look at important areas of business. These were:

- *Members trading services* – to provide professional indemnity, insurance, credit checks on prospects and debt collection services for members, and to obtain group purchasing discounts on legal services, travel and medical care.
- *Information services* – to help potential clients to identify design resources, to prepare a directory of members, to exchange information with other professional and trade bodies, and to prepare data for members on copyright and employment law.
- *Business standards* – to establish a code of practice, to formulate common approach on copyright, fees, commissions, presenting work and competitions, to encourage high standards through award schemes, and to organize training and seminars.
- *External relations* – to manage a design awareness programme, to carry out political lobbying, to introduce design into business management training, and to create links with the Institute of Directors and the marketing societies.
- *Business development* – to set up major design conferences, events and exhibitions, and to develop design management courses with the Open University.

Developments like these confirm the feeling in the 1980s that the design industry is going through a period of important change. Projects are on an increasingly larger scale and consultancies are growing with them, designers are learning to deal with the impact of technology and responding to the new level of interest from government and industry. The designers who make the most of these opportunities will be those who manage their resources best.

So how have the designers of the 1980s responded to the challenge? Already, there are consultancies – large and small – providing every aspect of design – graphics, packaging, book covers, product design, retail interiors, architecture, exhibitions, audio visual, corporate identity and many more specialist disciplines. Fast growing public consultancies are moving into unexpected areas like public relations and corporate advertising, operating under the wider umbrella of communications consultancies.

Yet, for the great majority, the business is a small one, and there are plenty of success stories to tell about the newcomers. While *Creative Review* was reporting Wolff Olins' thoughts on the future direction of a public design group, articles in the same issue discussed the prospects for a small Fitch breakaway and the success of a small partnership that had just completed a major packaging project for a bluechip company. A later issue discussed the implications of the changes in financial marketing for the design industry. The Midland Bank was quoted as saying its workload was too great for one design group; the Listening Bank was anxious to build up a portfolio of designers, large and small.

The diversity of the business has its origins in design history. In the 1950s, no one was quite sure what a design consultancy was supposed to do. The commercial artist and the advertising agent were still alive and well, but the graphic designer was a new phenomenon. The late Bill Morgan was a founding partner of French Morgan Thomson, one of the first design consultancies to be set up in London. He recalled how they had to explain to clients the services they could offer and how they should be briefed. The absence of an established design industry did make marketing easier. Morgan recalled how the consultancy got its first clients by placing an advertisement in *The Daily Telegraph*, saying that French Morgan Thomson still had the capacity to take on one or two more exclusive clients. The advertisement gave the consultancy the start it needed by producing four clients who formed the basis of the business for a long time to come.

The first real signs of a recognition of design came in the late 1960s when the big names like Pentagram, Michael Peters and Wolff Olins had their origins. At the same time, advertising agencies were flirting with the concept of full service – offering design as part of an overall package to clients. Their design service concentrated on exhibitions, packaging and publications. Although the agencies' intervention did not cause serious damage to the design industry, it may have helped to raise general awareness of design. The agency flirtation was short-lived though – full service, in many cases, made little contribution to agency profitability. Some of the agency design departments were allowed to die quietly, while others became independent subsidiaries. Purchasepoint, for example, was set up as a subsidiary of a large agency to handle point-of-sale and retail promotion. But, in a second move, some of the members of Purchasepoint split again to set up Design In Action, a consultancy specializing in publications and packaging.

Other factors were helping to build the demand for professional design services. The packaging industry was on the move; new technology and new materials laid the technical base for exciting graphics, while fierce competition and a close look at all elements of the product mix provided the marketing impetus. Much of Michael Peters' early creative output was packaging work, and this has continued as the central activity of the group. At the same time, there was a growing awareness of the importance of design to the retailer. Retail design became a dynamic growth sector with Habitat as the original trendsetters, but with plenty of activity among the smaller hot shops and even among slumbering giants like the Burton group with its design-led moves into Top Shop and Top Man. Fitch built its reputation in retail design, and when Fitch breakaway groups set up in the 1980s, it came as no real surprise that they took on retail accounts. The 1960s and 1970s also saw industrial reorganization on a large scale, with an increasing number of takeovers and mergers, and the appearance of large conglomerates. What these new industrial groups faced, apart from their internal problems of reorganization, was a crisis of identity – famous trading names and leading brands were in danger of disappearing into faceless conglomerates. And what were customers, suppliers and employees alike to make of the new groups? Establishing the corporate identity became a key task for the new board. Design was to play a leading role in corporate communications, and the discipline brought a new scale of operations to the design business.

By this time, some of the longer established consultancies were extending their activities into product and architectural design. Pentagram, from its earliest days, was an amalgam of talents: five partners with strong individual reputations in graphics, product design and architecture. The group was not offering everything to everyman, but developing excellence in each aspect of its business. As they discussed in their book, *Living by Design*, this was not simply a case of bolting on design to these sectors, but of seeing design as an essential part of the process (see also Chapter 6, page 96). Throughout the 1970s, the design business took on an increasingly diverse appearance, with the bigger groups growing bigger and small consultancies continuing to prove that small can be successful. Certainly by the end of the period, the main divisions were well marked, even if no one stuck rigidly to them. The scene in the 1980s is as diverse, with the main change in direction coming from the large consultancies who have gone public. While this trend is unlikely to affect the shape of the rest of the design business, the management skills and expertise needed to deal wtih larger organizations and more complex projects are likely to spill over into the smaller design practices. The scene in the mid 1980s is still that of a variegated design industry with a healthy number of new entrants.

This growing interest in management is not to suggest that designers should immediately hang up their Rapidographs and enrol for a management course. That is not the nature of the business. Far better to aim at a form of invisible management – one in which designers are aware of the way their businesses run, and in control of the factors that affect their success. *Design Week*'s 1986 survey of forty companies that had recently gone public highlights some of the important tasks designers face. These are some of the attitudes that are held and, with them, some suggested remedies:

- Britain lags behind Europe in recognizing the importance of design.
  Remedy: an industry-wide public relations campaign.
- Eighty-five per cent believe design is important to their business.
  Remedy: individual marketing effort to identify and sell to those prospects.
- Eighty per cent want to improve design input as a major part of their marketing strategy.
  Remedy: more education in client design management.
- Qualities looked for in a design consultancy are creativity, cost control, receptive personality and business grounding.
  Remedy: improved consultancy management skills.
- Belief that designers need to be better trained for industry and a low expectation of their business skills
  Remedy: improved consultancy management skills.
- Word of mouth is the most common way clients learn about a design consultancy.
  Remedy: stronger marketing communications.
- Fifty per cent had trouble with design consultancies, especially over cost control and understanding the brief.
  Remedy: improved business management and financial control.
- Only ten per cent regard design as more important than advertising.
  Remedy: a need for public relations to improve perception of design.
- Only twenty-five per cent represent design at board level through marketing.
  Remedy: a need for better client design management education.

- Only ten per cent have benefitted directly from the government drive to promote design in industry.
  Remedy: improve generic support for design.

Effective management will help designers overcome those attitudes and make the most of the new opportunities.

Management disciplines

Planning and control

The first step in managing your business is to plan your activities so that you know where you are going and how you are going to get there. A lack of planning and control can lead to chaos; you don't know what resources you need, how much money you need to keep the business running, how many staff you need to handle work, or even how much work you will have. The more of these factors you can control, the easier it will be to manage your business.

Planning is the discipline of achieving this. It means writing down your aims, all the factors that can affect your business and the resources you will need to run that business effectively. Planning should be done on a short- and long-term basis (see also chapter 6). Long-term planning helps to establish the future direction of the business and sets a series of intermediate targets that have to be achieved to reach the long-term objective. Short-term planning helps to tackle the immediate problems that face the consultancy in the coming weeks, months or years.

Chapter 6 dealing with expansion shows the many different objectives which can be set.

Control is closely linked to planning; plans are useless if they are just ideas on paper that are disregarded in the day-to-day running of the business. Plans should have targets that are realistic and they should be given to individuals as well as to the whole practice; this helps to involve other people in the running of the business. You should carry out regular checks to see that the targets are being met. For example, if the plan calls for a total income of £100,000 per year, the monthly target must be at least £9000. If monthly income falls below that, you need higher sales – the marketing plan has to be changed. If income falls below that figure continuously, the financial target may have to be reduced with possible effects on employment and the future growth of the business. Control allows you to make adjustments to your plans, while still keeping within the framework of your long-term objectives.

The disciplines of planning and control are also essential to other aspects of business management – marketing, finance, project management, personnel and administration.

Marketing

Marketing is the discipline of matching the practice's resources to market demand. Marketing should not be confused with selling; selling is part of the marketing process. Selling is finding prospects and persuading them that your service is what they need. Marketing is more fundamental – identifying clients' needs and providing the type of service that meets those needs. The skills of research are needed to identify the market and the prospects; product development skills are needed to formulate a service that meets the requirements; communications skills are needed to convey information on the service to the right prospects; pricing skills are needed to establish the right rate for the job; and selling skills are needed to close the deal. Chapter 2 describes these necessary skills.

Marketing has other important values; it is a management discipline that is used to run the business, but it is also a service that is increasingly offered to clients as part of a multidisciplinary design programme.

Finance

Finance is the crucial discipline of small business management – surveys show that the majority of small business failures are due to poor financial control. If a business does not generate enough profit, it cannot cover its costs, or provide the funds for growth and expansion. Financial management is not just the responsibility of accountants; designers have to make sure that their clients pay on time, they negotiate with suppliers, and they have to understand what expansion means. Financial management is the discipline of recording the income and expenditure of the consultancy, analysing it to see what action needs to be taken and looking forward to forecast and provide the future financial requirements of the business.

Chapter 3 on financial management describes the process in more detail.

Personnel

People are the most important part of a design business. Although most studios boast a relaxed informal atmosphere, personnel management does have an important part to play. There are legal obligations to staff – the Employment Act, for example, has regulations that affect your employees. You also need to motivate your staff and supervise their work to make sure that both parties are getting the best from their work.

Chapter 4 describes the important elements of personnel management.

Administration

Administration is sometimes confused with management: administration deals with specific tasks – handling a project, ordering goods from a supplier, dealing with clients or maintaining records. Sound administration is an important part of consultancy management, but does not involve the essential disciplines of planning and control.

Chapter 5 describes administrative skills related to project management, while Chapter 4 on personnel management describes how new technology can be used to improve administration and other aspects of management.

Management training

A formal system of management training for the design business is beiginning to emerge; there are independent courses on finance, organization and aspects of planning and control that are run as workshops with speakers from the design practices giving details of their practical experience. The London Enterprise Board runs courses in small business management including one on the management of a design practice. Although few art colleges include formal management studies in their courses there are moves to change this, and a proposal to include management studies in the BTEC course on design is likely to be implemented in the late 1980s. (See also Chapter 4, page 67.)

Design management training

To reflect the increasing emphasis on effective design management in the client company, professional and private organizations are running seminars and training courses. Their aim is to relate design to the disciplines of marketing, engineering and production management, and to promote the necessary links. Design management is likely to be available as a degree course in the late 1980s, and this should lead to a better informed client base.

Other areas of management training

There are a wide variety of general management courses for small businesses which are not geared specifically to the designer. These cover the principles of management and may, in some cases, be relevant. They range from introductory courses for the newly self-employed to foundation courses run by specialist management colleges. The London Business School runs a postgraduate course in small business management. In general, the more specific the course, the more valuable it will be.

Attitudes to the design business

Client surveys

Recent surveys among users of design show that designers have to overcome problems in a number of areas if their businesses are to succeed. Although there are problems that face the whole design business, action by individual consultants can do much to improve their own reputation with clients. Among the principle areas of client concern were cost control where final invoices bore little relation to estimates, a lack of professionalism and attention to detail in project control, a lack of understanding of the client's business objectives as these were translated into a design brief, and difficulty in seeing the client's point of view. Surveys like these can act as a checklist for your consultancy to see whether any of the comments apply to your business. If they do you need to take action.

The sections on pp. 9–10 describe a *Design Week* survey into client attitudes and suggests a number of courses of action.

Improving awareness of design

While the individual consultancy can do much to improve clients' awareness of design and its values, a far greater effort is needed from the design business. Well-informed clients contribute to a better educated market place and remove one stage from the selling process. The Design Council itself has done much to raise awareness with its permanent display of well-designed products at the Design Centre, as well as its Designer Selection Service and the Design Council Awards scheme. The Design Business Group has set an increasing awareness of design's potential as one of its principle objectives; among its planned activities are exhibitions, a press information programme and seminars aimed at influential design buyers.

The government believes design can be a valuable part of Britain's economic recovery and has set up a number of schemes to encourage greater use of design services. Support for Design, formerly the Funded Consultancy Scheme, provides an introduction to design for potential clients; they receive a specified number of days' free consulatncy, with more at a reduced fee. The Design Council, which runs the scheme for the Department of Trade and Industry, pays the balance of the fee to the consultancy. An annual meeting at Downing Street, chaired by the Prime Minister, brought together industrialists, designers and politicians, who, it was believed, had common interests (see Chapter 2, page 25).

Development of design

Design consultancies developed as a recognizable business in the 1950s, although there had been individuals working in private practice for many years. The main design activity in the early stages was graphic design, popularly known as commercial art. Product design was an engineering-based profession, although the Council for Industrial Design had some early influence on product design in the late 1950s. Interior design was then a distinct branch of architecture. The business began to assume its current shape in the 1960s. Pentagram was perhaps the typical sixties consultancy, founded by partners with different but complementary backgrounds in architecture, graphics and product design. Michael Peters made his first appearance as a packaging designer and Conran Design began work with the Habitat Catalogue.

Design grew as a business throughout the 1970s fending off competition from full service advertising agencies among others, but strong growth came in the 1980s with the development of retail and product design. There had been a handful of large successful consultancies, but the important change came with the large-scale national projects to redesign whole chains of retail outlets. This demanded teams of designers working on extended projects or on projects that had to be completed quickly. This new business demanded other skills beyond basic design or beyond the core skill of the consultancy.

A retail design project, for example, would require graphics, marketing, interior design and architecture, as well as significant project management skills. Packaging design was closely linked to product design and it too benefitted from the disciplines of marketing and graphics.

At the same time, there was a movement to recognize the value of design for its own sake and to curb the trend towards design as big business. There were successful small consultancies who believed that the quality of design was more important than the drive for profit forced on the public consultancies.

Surveys indicated that the design business of the 1980s was a growing diversified business which had room for the independent designer as well as the very large consultancy.

Structure of the design business

A classification of design is a useful starting point for analysing the business and planning your own future direction.

Design disciplines

Graphic designers   design information – how images are perceived in relation to their environment and their function. Their work is diverse and can be found in publications, corporate identity, packaging, display, exhibitions, signing and the visual appearance of stores and buildings. Graphic designers often work as part of a multidisciplinary team on certain types of project – product or retail development, for example.

Product designers   design products. Their involvement could be comprehensive where they provide concept, prototype, specification and production details for a new product, or it could be ad hoc, where they consider specific aspects of an existing product such as operation, style, value engineering or production engineereing. The product designer incorporates the skills of an engineering designer, stylist and production engineer.

Architectural designers   live on a professional borderline between architecture and design; they consider the design elements of buildings. Although they may not be responsible for the overall structural and functional design, they can help clients by offering advice and service on the appearance and development of retail outlets.

Interior designers   also work in retail where they design the layout, appearance and fitting of the store. Their role is much wider, taking in interior design of offices, domestic and public buildings.

Exhibition designers   specialize in the design of exhibition stands. There is some overlap in this area with graphic designers who may include exhibition design among their services.

Other classifications are more specialized: textile designers and fashion designers provide a design service to the clothing industry; audio-visual designers specialize in the design and production management of audio-visual programmes – this is another area where the graphic designer offers a similar service. A number of other areas of graphic design are offered as specialist services: corporate identity, packaging and publications.

These are the main functional areas of design. The skills and the services are often combined in one designer or consultancy and, as the classification showed, there is often an overlap in the services available to solve a particular design problem. Retail design, for example, is a recognized commercial service although it embraces a number of different design disciplines and has no separate professional organization.

Consultancy or individual

Design is a business that depends on individual skills as much as company resources; size is therefore no indication of the quality of service that is available. A survey in the magazine *Design Week* showed the enormous variation between the small group of large consultancies whose staff numbered hundreds and the very large number with less than ten employees. Yet, if you compared information on the same designers' clients, it is possible to find practices at both ends of the scale working for blue chip clients. The difference may be in the scale of project that consultancies can handle and the skills and resources they can provide. For the client, the selection process is therefore a matter of matching requirements with resources. Individual designers offer their own personal skills; any other resources they have to buy in and manage. An individual designer can have experience and qualifications in any of the areas of design practice; he may work in number of areas to ensure continuity of work, or he may provide a specialist service in one area of design (see also Chapter 2, page 23).

Scale of design practices

A design practice in the current market can range in size from two employees to some six hundred. Not all of these employees may be designers; a practice needs support and administrative staff as well as other professionals, and some of them may help to meet your requirements. A practice can specialize in a single activity – graphics, retail, packaging, architecture – or it may offer a spread of services, bringing together the right team for the project. These services may be offered through one company or they may be available through specialist divisions or companies within a group.

Little has been done to survey the design business; the Chartered Society of Designers publishes a directory of members showing designers in individual practice as well as those members who work in consultancies. The Design Business Group was planning to create a register of its members who were, in the main, working in consultancies. The Design Council maintains a register of designers but this is an information service to design clients rather than a comprehensive register.

An independent survey by the magazine *Design Week* listed the leading consultancies and numbers of employees. This did not cover all consultancies, only those who had responded to the survey. *Design Week*'s survey of the top one hundred UK design consultancies showed a remarkable spread of employees. At the top of the list were a small group of multidisciplinary consultancies who employed up to five hundred people; one of their main disciplines was architecture and their growth has been largely based on acquisitions and mergers. A small number of consultancies had over one hundred employees, but the majority of what could be considered large consultancies employed between thirty and fifty people. Below that came a very large group of consultancies with less than ten employees, and it was actually possible to get into the top one hundred with just four employees. If you added to that the numbers of individual designers, the scene is of a very diverse business.

Diversification in design

During the 1980s, a small number of the larger consultancies became public companies on the Unlisted Securities Market; the trend in these consultancies was to structure their companies to offer specialist services separately. Another trend is for design practices to diversify their activities away from pure design to set up satellite companies offering related services. Wolff Olins – which initially specialized in corporate identity – set up companies offering corporate public relations and corporate advertising so that they could meet all their clients' corporate communications requirements. A growing number of design consultancies are forming associations with market research or marketing consultancies to offer a one-stop service to clients.

A design practice can also be a constituent part of a communications or management group; the parent group may acquire an existing practice or set up a new operation. The international advertising agency WCRS bought Beresford Design and a number of other specialist companies to establish a communications group. Saatchi and Saatchi, on the other hand, set up a design practice using their own resources, while PA Design was established as an autonomous division within the PA Consulting Group to specialize in product design and development. The division was later bought by the Michael Peters Group to strengthen its product design activities. Each of these design companies would be able to draw on the resources and complementary skills of other companies within the group when these were relevant to a project (see Chapter 6, page 100).

The types of practice described so far provide a full service within their own field of activity and work to professional standards. Design is also available from other types of supplier, though not necessarily to the same standards. Printers, for example, sometimes offer to carry out design as part of a total package for producing a publication. Packaging manufacturers can offer a studio service to handle the graphics. Advertising agencies at one stage in their development included design as part of a total service offer to clients, sometimes providing the service within the commission they earned from media advertising. Current agency practice is to put design on a proper commercial footing, and to offer the service through an associate company on a normal fee basis (see Chapter 2, page 30).

International design services

International design groups that can provide a global service for multinational clients are beginning to appear. The Design Network is part of an international group of associate companies who can provide clients with local service in a number of countries and extra resources to deal with overload of work. Other consultancies like Pentagram and Allied International Designers have associates in other countries. A number of overseas design practices have offices in the UK which provide a full service to British clients; the American group Landor Associates is among the best known of these and achieved a major coup when it carried out the redesign of British Airways' corporate identity.

Design resources

Size and structure are no guide to the quality of design services available from different suppliers. Like the relationship with an advertising agency or public relations consultancy, much depends on the quality of the people and the chemistry between consultant and client. A design practice has other resources that help it to achieve its business objectives – computerized design tools, associated services, support staff – but its primary skills are design and project management.

Information on the design business

Newspapers and magazines on design provide up-to-date information on who is doing what, and can, in some cases, provide more detailed information on the thinking behind the design work. Among newspapers, the most influential is *The Financial Times* where Christopher Lorenz writes a regular and well-respected column on design. The *Guardian* includes a section on media in its Monday issue and this gives an increasing amount of coverage to design. The number of magazines giving specialist or occasional coverage to design is increasing. The longest established is *Design* published monthly by the Design Council. It provides a news service showing what is new in design and includes case histories of design projects as well as features on individual designers and practices. The magazine publishes a regular listing of design services available under various classifications.

Design Week, which is the newest, has quickly established itself as the design business equivalent of *Campaign* or *Marketing*. It has a high news content with details of new design commissions and completed projects; like *Design*, it also includes case histories explaining the background to design solutions. An interesting new development in *Design Week* is the Design Leads service. This is a service that is free to clients who want design services; they place a brief summary of the service they need in the column and invite proposals for design services.

Two other magazines cover design, though not to the same level. *Creative*

Review and *Design and Art Direction* are monthlies which provide a news and feature service on the creative services business, covering design, advertising, illustraton, photography and related services. *Campaign*, the weekly magazine of the advertising business, carries news of the design business and publishes occasional feature articles on design. *Marketing* magazine also publishes regular features on product and packaging design relating design work to practical marketing problems. *Graphics World*, published bimonthly, is a relatively small circulation magazine which follows the contents format of the other design magazines.

Design magazines can help you keep up to date with the design buisness and give you a picture of the relative positions of other consultancies. There is a growing collection of books on design that can provide an introduction to the business and its contributors. Existing literature has tended to concentrate on product design and has unfortunately not related it to the design process, but these books are helping to raise awareness of the value of design. Christopher Lorenz's book *The Design Dimension* takes a close look at the way companies have used design to improve their competitive position; he provides many examples of the way large and small companies have used design and discusses the practical implementation of design. Pentagram's book *Living By Design* gives a valuable insight into the designer at work. The book looks at the work of the practice and explains the thinking behind large and small design projects.

In parallel with the growth of books and magazines, there has been an increase in the number of seminars and conferences dealing with design and marketing. The British Institute of Management ran one recently with the title Design and Marketing, and the Design Business Group plans to run a significant programme of client education. You can find details of these seminars in *Marketing*, *Design Week* and *Design*.

Factors affecting the development of design

Businesses rise or fall with the general level of economic activity, and anyone looking at the long-term prospects of their business has to consider economic factors. But there are a number of factors relating to design that can be considered separately. Awareness of design has grown considerably, partially through government efforts and partly through a recognition of the contribution that design can make to business development generally. Design is now seen as an important part of the marketing process. The growth of professional consultancies and the formation of the Design Business Group confirmed these developments.

Growth in design's main markets is another important factor. As a service industry, design is affected by trends in its own customer industries. The boom in high street retail development, for example, may have passed its peak but there is a growing interest in the refurbishment of out-of-town retail centres. Corporate identity too, which hit a peak in the 1970s, is now coming up for a second round of overhauls and new identities. The financial market has grown rapidly following the deregulation of the City in 1986 and the Building Societies Act. Interest in product design is growing steadily but has shown no real peaks or dramatic surges like retail. Much depends on the professionalism of the client; developments in the acceptance of design management as a profession is likey to help design (see Chapter 2, page 34).

Business planning

Business objectives

Planning is essential to business management; as we showed at the beginning of this section, it helps you to keep your business under control and to make decisions that are relevant to your business objectives. Your objectives can take a number of different forms, including:

- To become the largest UK design consultancy
- To develop a global design business
- To make a personal fortune
- To win awards for good design
- To become the leading specialist in book design
- To raise your turnover by twenty-five per cent.
- To replace the three accounts that were lost last year.

As the list shows, objectives can be general or specific. The more specific they are, the easier they are to quantity. To reach long-term objectives, the plan needs to be broken down into smaller components. The overall plan should be seen as a series of steps each leading towards the goal. All your other decisions should be relevant. If your overall objective is to become the leading specialist book design consultancy, it would be off-target to recruit someone with retail experience. Anyone planning to build the largest UK consultancy has to make marketing decisions about the sort of business they will go for – ideally fast turnover, high volume clients with good growth prospects. Financial decisions are just as important as marketing decisions to anyone with global design aspirations. They have to fund the cost of start-up businesses around the world, and they may have to meet the cost of acquisitions or mergers with other companies.

Business audit

Audit is a technical term used primarily in finance and accounting, but it is also relevant to business planning. It is a way of assessing your business – seeing what skills and resources you have and how you stand in relation to the resources you will need to meet your business objectives. Auditing is often carried out on an informal basis, but it can be valuable to handle the exercise formally. The audit should begin with a statement of your business objectives and a list of the financial, marketing, personnel, technical and other resources that are needed to reach the targets. The audit would also show your strengths and weaknesses as a consultancy. If your strengths relate to your main business objectives, you are in a good position, but if there are weaknesses in important areas, it is time to eliminate them. This type of analysis is knwon as a SWOT analysis – strengths, weaknesses, opportunities and threats (from competitors).

Planning and implementation

The audit confirms the current status of the consultancy and the plan shows the way forward. Putting the business plan into action calls for different levels of detail planning in each of the subsidiary disciplines – marketing, personnel, finance and business support. Each of them will have its own specific targets, but they will have to be related to the overall plan. The marketing plan, for example, could call for the development of four new multinational accounts or the position of market leader in a specialist sector. Financial planning should be geared to the level of funding you will need for your expansion plans. If you think that new premises will be needed in the third year, then you need to provide money for that; if you are planning to acquire other companies, you will need to have substantial assets.

While intermediate targets may seem less important, they need careful attention; they are steps on the way to achieving your long-term objectives.

TWO
Marketing

Importance of marketing

Marketing has become a double-edged weapon for the designer: it is a management discipline that aims to increase the level of profitable business the practice handles; and, for the so-called marketing-led consultancies, it is providing a service to clients. In this section we are looking at marketing as a way of developing business.

One indication of marketing's growing importance is the increase in recruitment activity for design marketing staff. Traditionally, marketing or selling has been a responsibility of the senior partners – a task for which they are probably ill prepared. Where marketing has been confined to occasional contact or presentations to new prospects, this approach may well have been adequate, but to undertake a comprehensive marketing programme, the consultancy will need the support of professional marketing staff. Recognizing this need for professional design marketing staff, a number of recruitment consultancies have set up specialist divisions to meet the needs (see Chapter 4, page 69).

The larger consultancies have made a number of marketing staff appointments at senior level. Conran appointed a business development director – a senior appointment which reflected the importance of the position. Michael Peters had a marketing director as well as a public relations manager to handle press information. James Woodhuysen, former editor of *Design* magazine, was appointed as director of information at Fitch. Coley, Porter, Bell had built up their own strength in marketing as a client service; three of their board members had come from senior marketing positions in industry. They were able to add their expertise to the marketing of the company's own services.

Other consultancies – who had not yet appointed professional marketing staff – recognized the value of new business development because design is a business where ad hoc projects predominate. It is important to maintain long-term relationships with clients whenever possible, but it is also essential to build a broad client base. Arthur King of Arthur King & Associates stressed the importance of a continuous marketing effort. He felt that their business had grown naturally to a certain stage, but that to achieve further significant growth the consultancy would need to appoint someone with full-time responsibility for business development.

There is an equally important industry marketing task to be achieved, despite the currently high profile of design. The Design Business Group see one of their key tasks as promoting the value of design through a programme of exhibitions, seminars and press information. They are also trying to build a stronger base of research on prospects for design. To date there is little published information on the market for design services. Research is a valuable starting point for marketing planning; it provides an overall framework for the marketing effort and supplements research into individual prospects (see page 27). Research can be misleading though.

In 1985, any major design group that did not have an interest in retail work might have been considered short-sighted. Major new projects were announced every month; consultancy size seemed to be expanding geometrically, and success in retail was proving to be a springboard for a number of consultancies to go public. During 1986, a report on the retail market suggested that perhaps the boom was to be short lived. Many of the major projects had been completed and long-term growth would be slower – not good news for the faint hearted. Yet, a few months later, another survey pointed to dramatic new growth opportunities in the refurbishment and redevelopment of the country's shopping centres. Clearly the consultancies could go in a number of different directions.

Research should be used with caution. Research helps you identify key market sectors, but it can also help to shape the service you offer the client. Piper identified a need for a retail service that went further than the design service that was currently available. They developed a service that included store design but also looked at merchandise policy, training and products. Piper's service was valuable to clients who wanted to develop total retail concepts and implement them.

Product development is also the concept behind the rising number of communications groups. Design with marketing and advertising, and design with interiors and architecture were two of the favoured combinations (see Chapter 6, page 100). The strategy was to offer the client a service with greater depth, or a service that was integrated. Packaging, for example, is part of an overall communications strategy, and, in the mind of the consumer, it is closely linked to the advertising message. In an article in *What's New in Marketing*, Coley, Porter, Bell described some of the issues that packaging designers face – issues that they felt influenced the way they worked. Packaging works in the environment of the store; but the stores themselves are changing – some with a positive attitute to design, some relying on price as the only marketing weapon. Well-packaged products that have high consumer appeal can be used as a competitive weapon in the supermarket shelf war. Packaging should reflect and help to create consumer attitudes towards the product, so consumer research and testing plays an important part in establishing the image of the product. That image should also relate to the image portrayed in the advertising support for the product. It takes a range of skills to deal with packaging at this depth; within a communications group it is possible to put together a project team with all the right skills.

Product development can also be considered from the point of view of the scale of resources available. As Chapter 5 on project management will show, clients look to designers to provide the resources and the professionalism to complete projects on time and within budget. An article in *Design Week* on shopping centre redevelopment discussed the way developers – who are the clients on this type of project – preferred to ask one of a small group of design consultancies who had the size and the experience to handle work on this scale. Any consultancy that wants to work on large projects must give priority to developing resources to provide the right level of service.

Size is not always the only criterion for selection in retail design. As Peter Leonard Associates showed, clients like to work with consultancies they feel are hungry. Peter Leonard's breakthrough came on the WH Smith redesign; they beat several of the larger consultancies in a competitive pitch for the redesign of a pilot flagship branch, but then to everyone's surprise they were awarded the contract for the refurbishment of the national chain (see Chapter 5, page 75).

Size is usually an important factor – though size alone cannot guarantee a consultancy a place among the contenders. Clients and prospects have to be aware of your capabilities. McColl's decision to place a much greater emphasis on public relations was partly a reaction to an experience in a competitive pitch. In the final decision, the consultancy lost out, and the reason they were given was that they were not enough of a household name. Their answer was to set up a press information programme so that they got full marketing value from a successful project.

The obvious target for press information may seem to be the design press, but many observers feel this is taking an insular attitude. Design magazines are preaching to the converted – designers themselves and those clients who already believe in the value of design. This may have considerable value in its own right – professional design clients who believe in design may have a large work programme; they are looking for good suppliers and the design press is a natural place to look. Good coverage in the design press also has an important non-marketing role – helping to raise the profile of the consultancy within the industry, giving employees confidence in the consultancy and helping to attract good designers. The real emphasis, however, should be on the marketing value of press information. Press information should be aimed at the target market. Consultancies who market retail design services should aim their information at the retail business press; packaging specialists at a sector like food; product designers at the business or engineering management press.

Press information programmes should operate at three different levels: design awareness campaigns, capability programmes and service news. Design awareness campaigns help to make clients better informed; here the consultancy takes a back seat, but explains issues like the marketing benefits of good packaging design, the importance of a good design brief or the value of corporate identity. Articles like this help to increase the base for design services, but they also give the consultancy a degree of authority and this can help to build a reputation for professionalism. Wolff Olins and corporate identity have become almost synonymous, and that has much to do with Wally Olins' continuous efforts to stress the value of corporate identity – through articles in the design and business press, appearances at business seminars and books on the management of corporate identity programmes.

Capability programmes are also aimed at raising the professional status of the consultancies. Articles could describe new recruits, or new equipment that improves performance in a specific area – computer graphics to improve productivity, for example, or communications equipment that provides efficient links with clients and suppliers. Capability articles can also be built around particular projects that show a high degree of capability or special resources.

Services news improves awareness of consultancy capability, for example press releases that describe projects that have recently been completed. They show the areas where the consultancy operates and the scale of project it handles. Choice of medium is equally important here. A series of news stories in the design press would raise the profile of the consultancy, but the same releases in the target market press would help to increase market penetration.

Who is to handle press information, if it is so important? For the consultancy with a press officer or public relations/marketing director it is one of their responsibilities, but many consultancies do not have the resources or volume of news to warrant a full-time specialist. In business, inhouse public relations activity is supported by the services of a public relations consultancy. Like designers, they have areas of specialization and a small group of public relations professionals are now specializing in design. They believe that the design industry has made some bad marketing appointments – where the new recruit had the right professional qualifications, but did not have the experience of professional consulting services. The specialist design public relations consultancies work closely with the consultancy principals and help to set strategy, as well as carrying out the day-to-day work.

Advertising is another option for the consultancy that wants to raise its profile. Space budgets and the costs of advertising production have kept this to modest proportions. The design press continues to carry a high proportion of designer's advertising, but the same problems could apply to this type of advertising – that it is preaching to the converted. *Marketing*, *Marketing Week*, *Financial Decisions* and *Management Today* have been carrying examples of designer's advertising; here the advertising is clearly aimed at design decision-markers in marketing and other executive positions. There has been a tendency to concentrate on corporate advertising where the advertisement shows a series of recently completed design projects or a list of client names. Neither format carries any original advertising concepts though it is not surprising when low expenditure restricts campaigns to do-it-yourself advertising. Advertising agencies provide a specialist service in media planning and creative work, but they work on commission from the space they buy for the advertiser, and this is unlikely to be high (see page 36).

With the increasing interest in design, there are many opportunities to speak at seminars. Recently the Marketing Society, Confederation of British Industry, Department of Trade and Industry, and the TUC have presented seminars on different aspects of design. The speakers have included representatives from both sides – industry and the professions. This gives the consultancy the opportunity to demonstrate professionalism and the chance to meet design clients. Exhibitions too bring suppliers and clients together – although the medium is not yet fully developed for the design business. The Design Business Group saw exhibitions as a way of bringing the two parties together, and there were efforts in 1987 to set up the first national exhibition of design services. The first exhibition was cancelled because the time seemed too short to make proper preparations, but the show looks set to become an annual event. Freelance designers and suppliers to the design business had their own exhibition in 1987 – the Freelance Services Exhibition. Exhibitions – like advertising and press relations – should be used with caution; they should be aimed at the right target market.

Despite the gradual acceptance of new promotional media like advertising, press relations, seminars and exhibitions, direct mail and the consultancy brochure remain the long-standing favourites. There are few consultancies that have not produced their own brochure – listing clients, showing examples of work they have done and stating their corporate philosophy.

The format of the brochures varies widely and often reflects the type of work the consultancy handles. Consultancies that handle a small group of large projects use a traditional corporate brochure approach – bound material; practices that turn over projects quickly have favoured a loose leaf approach, inserting individual cards in a folder. The amount of supporting copy also varies. In a brochure provided by one of the marketing-led consultancies, there was a strong emphasis on the marketing background to a project and a statement of the consultancy's approach to marketing; graphics predominated in the brochures from practices specializing in publications and packaging.

Public consultancies have an additional opportunity to demonstrate their design abilities through the annual report to shareholders. Michael Peters produced a special pop-up report to demonstrate the work of a design group and to make an effective presentation of their results.

Promotional techniques such as those described in the preceding sections are used to develop new business by attracting prospects who might not be fully committed to design, or to win business against competition. You also need to keep yourself in contention when clients are actively looking for a design consultancy. The Design Council Selection Service is one source of information for clients. The Design Council compiles a register of designers listing their specific skills; the skills are coded for easy reference and the designer can supply supporting material in the form of slides or samples of work. The client specifies the skills he needs and is given a shortlist of suitable consultancies to evaluate. *Design Week* magazine runs a 'design leads' service. Clients outline the project they are planning and designers are asked to contact the client directly or through a box number. The majority of projects so far have looked more suitable for freelance designers or small consultancies – one-off projects rather than major exercises.

A more ambitious project to bring clients and designers together is Support for Design. It began life as the Funded Consultancy Scheme, and its objective was to encourage prospective clients to sample design without full financial commitment. Under the scheme, the client gets a specified number of days free consultancy, with a follow-on period at a reduced rate. The consultancy is paid at an agreed rate by the Design Council which is administering the scheme for the government. The Design Council's initial report on the scheme indicated that the main subscribers were larger organizations who were trying out product design services. In the second phase – Support for Design – the scheme was aimed at a wider spread of businesses and encouraged them to make use of the full range of design services. Preliminary reports suggested that smaller companies were taking up the opportunity and that areas like graphics and packaging now received more attention.

There was a mixed reaction from the design consultancies who had been involved in the scheme; some felt that it was very time consuming in relation to normal commercial work – clients wanted to get as much from the service as they could. Others felt that the scheme provided work they would not have had otherwise. Critics of the scheme focused on the fact that it gave support to profitable companies who could well afford normal design fees. However, the scheme's main objectives were to increase the acceptance of design not to provide financial aid, so the objections were irrelevant.

A recent growth area in marketing services for designers is the design agency; the service is suitable for freelance designers and small consultancies, and operates like an illustration agency. The agency takes over marketing and administration, leaving the designer free to concentrate on design.

Gamble Grey was set up in the 1980s to provide this type of service; the agency worked with a small group of designers whose work they felt was complementary and exciting. On larger, more complex projects they were able to bring together teams of designers who could provide the resources that individuals were unable to match, and added their own project management skills to the specialist design skills. The agency was able to provide the people on its books with greater continuity of work and, in return, they took a percentage of the design fee as their management charge. There were no long-term commitments between the two parties, however; both recognized that success and growth were natural and that the small practice would develop naturally into a successful independent consultancy.

Whatever form of marketing support a consultancy employs to develop its business, it still faces strong competition in the marketplace. Price competition is one of the most difficult problems to contend with (see Chapter 3, page 47). Design is not a commodity that is bought on price alone; quality and the effectiveness of the solution are by far the strongest selling points a consultancy can have, but increasingly clients are demanding a basis for comparison. In the absence of an established fee scale, there is little that an individual consultancy can do about it. It must develop other marketing strengths.

Marketing design services

Design is a service that can only be demonstrated when a client has a problem to solve. Design cannot be bought off the shelf, although the results of the design process can be seen in the shape of products, packaging, leaflets, and the shelves and retail outlets themselves. Clients are not buying those completed products, they are buying the skills and the service to help create a product.

Under strict professional rules, the onus is on the client to find the right designer to meet his needs. The designer would not be allowed to solicit for business. But in a commercial and competitive environment, marketing is an essential task for the designer. The process should not be confused with selling; selling is simply the persuasive stage in marketing – the stage at which the designer convinces the prospect that his is the right service to use. Even when the client approaches the designer, the designer has to convince the client that he has the qualifications, experience, skills and understanding to solve the client's problems. That is the selling process.

Marketing is an approach to business; it begins by identifying profitable markets and prospects for design services – what type of business or organization needs design services, who are they, where are they and how many of them are there? It asks what type of design services they need – how often do they use it and in what form it is delivered? Marketing brings prospects and suppliers together by a process of communication. The selling process only begins when the right client and supplier have come together. Marketing does not stop at the sale – customer service and follow-up can help to build continuity of business. Marketing can have a fundamental effect on the nature of a design business – it should determine the design services that are offered, the qualifications and skills of future employees, the equipment that is bought, and the long-term plans of the business (see Chapter 1, page 10).

In other words, what resources will be needed to provide the services – how many designers, what qualifications should they have, what other types of staff will be needed, who will be the key suppliers?. Like any other aspect of business management, marketing should begin with a plan. Its essential elements are:

- Research programme to identify key market sectors and prospects
- Marketing objectives to set the targets for turnover and market penetration
- Marketing communications programme
- Marketing resources – staff, communications, budget, marketing support material.

Research

Research points the marketing effort in the right direction. It should help to identify the important market areas and the key prospects for a design service. A comprehensive research programme can provide many different types of information about the market for design including:

- *The size of the market* – in expenditure and in numbers of prospects.
- *Growth of the market* – increase or decrease in expenditure over a period of time.
- *Key sectors* – by size or by growth.
- *Purchasing information* – who the prospects are, where they are located and how much they are spending.
- *Prospect information* – who makes the decision to buy design services and who selects the consultancy.
- *Competitive activity* – who is already selling to the market and what is their share.
- *Purchasing factors* – what are buyers looking for in a design consultancy.

Research can take a number of different forms:

- *Published surveys* – surveys carried out by government departments, research companies, professional institutes or other design companies are often available. The information may not be specific to what you need to know, but it can help to establish a direction for your own research.
- *Directory information* – directories are published covering many different industries; they are unlikely to give any clues to design purchasing potential, but they can help to quantify information about key industries or individual prospects.
- *Commissioned research* – a research consultancy can carry out research to a specific brief.

The Market Research Society publish a directory of members and the services they offer.

Markets for design services

This section looks at the opportunities for business in the main design categories, shows their source of work and the skills that are required. In a later section we look in more detail at these factors in relation to graphic design.

Graphic design

Projects

Publications – sales leaflets/brochures, corporate brochures, annual reports, catalogues, mail shots, house magazines, user manuals, training manuals, staff literature, technical handbooks.

Sources of work – direct from clients or through advertising agencies and public relations consultancies with no design facilities.

Stationery and information systems – letterheads, forms, delivery notes and other documents to conform to corporate style, or to simplify paperwork.

Sources of work – direct from client, especially larger companies handling complicated business.

Editorial design – magazine layout, newspaper design, design of mastheads/covers, grid design, book covers.

Sources of work – publishers, editors, editorial consultancies.

Important sectors – financial, high technology, corporate.

Complementary skills – writing, production management, photography, illustration.

Packaging design

Projects – packaging design or redesign, range packaging, packaging graphics, functional design, application of corporate identify.

Sources of work – direct from clients, through advertising agencies, packaging manufacturers/printers, retailer's own label.

Important sectors – food, cosmetics, wines and spirits, stationery, do-it-yourself, own label, confectionery.

Complementary skills – marketing, packaging technology, retail.

Retail design

Projects – store refurbishment, department refurbishment, new store, shopping centre design and graphics, refurbishment of chain of stores, merchandizing/dispay/point-of-sale, store graphics, merchandise/packaging design, store identity.

Sources of work – direct from retailers, property owners, property developers, architects, interior designers.

Important sectors – high street retailers, own label, shopping centres, petrol stations.

Complementary skills – marketing, graphics, architecture, interiors, display.

Interior design

Projects – office design/refurbishment, retail projects, domestic projects, exhibition work.

Sources of work – direct from client (corporate and individual), architects, exhibition contractors, property owners/developers.

Important sectors – financial, retail.

Complementary skills – architecture, graphics, retail.

Product design

Projects – new product development and design, ergonomic design, product redesign, product styling, production engineering consultancy.

Sources of work – direct to client, advertising agencies, management and marketing consultancies.

Important sectors – high technology products, consumer products.

Complementary skills – engineering, marketing, modelmaking, ergonomics.

Exhibition design

Projects – stand design, shell scheme design, exhibition concepts, display, exhibition graphics, exhibition support material.

Sources of work – direct from client, exhibition organizers/contractors, advertising agencies.

Complementary skills – graphics.

Corporate identity design

Projects – logos, corporate identity recommendations/implementation, updating corporate identity.

Sources of work – direct from client, public relations consultancy, advertising agencies.

Important sectors – financial, professional, mergers.

Complementary skills – graphics, marketing.

Competition for design consultancies

Competition comes from advertising agencies, printers, public relations consultancies, and specialist suppliers of audio-visual, exhibitions and packaging. Some may include a nominal design service as part of a comprehensive sales package to a prospect, while others offer design as an integral part of their service and employ qualified designers. The consultancy also faces indirect competition from the staff designer or the do-it-yourself client. There was a trend in the 1970s for advertising agencies to offer an all-embracing range of marketing and promotional services to their clients; they were known as full-service agencies. For reasons of professionalism or profitability, most of them found the business too hot to handle, and they either dropped the service or set it up as an independent activity to fade or prosper quietly. The practice has now turned full circle, so that advertising agencies have become important buyers of design services, and the distinction between clients and competitors is blurred.

This brief list of competitors shows the other types of supplier who offer design services:

Graphics	Printers, agencies, public relations consultancies
Packaging	Packaging manufacturers, printers, advertising agencies

Corporate identity	Advertising agencies, public relations consultancies
Interiors	Architects
Product	Manufacturers
Retail	Architects, shopfitters
Exhibitions	Systems manufacturers, contractors, advertising agencies

The marketing task is to analyse the service offered by these competitors and identify your own strengths.

Trends in the market for graphic design services

Unless you specialize in working for government or the professions, the bulk of your work is likely to come from business. Not all businesses have, or realize they have, a need for design services. You need to identify the better prospects; they include companies with technical or complex products, companies with large dealer networks, and companies with a complex operating structure. What they all have in common is a need to impart large amounts of information to dealers and prospective customers, investors and employees.

Technical products

Companies with technical products, such as computers, have to supply a great deal of information before and after a sale. The decision to buy a technical product is a complex one, involving a number of different decision-makers. Separate sales literature would be prepared to inform an executive, departmental manager, user and a data processing professional. Each needs different information, so the designer's task is to create a literature system that meets those different objectives, yet retains a strong corporate image. After the sale the company has a responsibility to supply clear, easy-to-follow user guides and instruction manuals, which should follow the corporate style. In this fast-moving market, new product releases are frequent, so there is a continuous demand for literature.

The computer industry is a prime prospect, but there are similar high technology developments in other industries, including printing equipment, machine tools, electronics components, control systems, security, process engineering, office equipment and telecommunications. Even if the traditional engineering industry has been left behind by the technological revolution, it still represents an important market for designers. Companies who make technical products produce a variety of sales literature, data sheets, catalogues and instruction manuals. Though the products change less frequently, they still require a high volume of publications.

As you move along the technical spectrum towards consumer products, the demand for extensive product literature becomes lower; companies who market their products to industry spend a much higher proportion of their budgets on literature, while consumer goods companies tend to allocate their budget to press and television advertising.

Dealer networked products

One area where there is little distinction is products that are sold through a dealer network. Here the person selling the products is one step removed from the company, and may not have sufficient product knowledge to sell effectively. For that reason companies in both consumer and industrial markets run dealer support programmes. These consist of training material, such as handbooks, market and product guides, as well as display and sales aids.

In the consumer sector the products might include electrical goods such as hi-fi, cars, home computers, and home improvement products – products that cannot simply be sold off the shelf. In the industrial sector companies who sell components, service parts, materials or disposable goods such as lubricants through a dealer network need the same kind of support material.

Large organizations

The third type of important prospect is the large organization with many employees, scattered locations and diverse operating companies. Here there are two opportunities: one is to handle the corporate activities such as annual reports, corporate brochures, and corporate identity programes; the other opportunity is to get involved in employee relations programmes. In a very large organization not all employees will be aware of developments and activities in the rest of the group. It is important to keep everyone informed, so companies produce newspapers, magazines, audio-visual programmes, and other forms of employee communications.

Financial and professional services sector

These two important new markets for graphic design have emerged recently. In both cases, changes in the regulations on competition and new business development have given firms the freedom and the commercial incentive to set up strong marketing operations. Accountancy firms, for example, have extensive programmes of promotional and information literature to describe the diversifying range of services they now offer clients. In the financial services sector, the 'Big Bang' of 1986, which changed the way the Stock Exchange and its members operated, led to a large number of mergers and a strong growth in publicity material about the services that were now available.

Contacts within an organization

Who you contact within an organization depends on the type of design work you want to handle and the size and structure of the organization. The important considerations are that the person you deal with has the authority to initiate the project, put adequate resources behind it, and has the drive and weight to get approvals at the right level. In most cases this would be the professional handling the project on a day-to-day basis, but a major project like a national retail redesign would need the authority of someone at board level to support and steer the project.

Contacts for graphic design services

Graphic design has traditionally been managed within a client company in the same way as advertising and public relations, and here there are a number of possible contacts.

In business, publicity managers are a good starting point. They control publicity budgets and are responsible for all of a company's promotional activities. Titles vary with company practice or specialization. The same person, with wide ranging responsibilities, can be called an advertising manager, sales promotion manager, public relations or public affairs manager, marketing services manager, or head of communications. In smaller companies this could be one of the many responsibilities of the sales, technical or marketing manager. Larger companies, with professional attitudes towards design and communications and budgets to match, set up departments of people who specialize in different disciplines. You could find publications advisers, heads of design, print managers, exhibition or audio-visual managers. They, in turn, may handle projects for only part of the company. In a large group with many different constituent companies and locations, there may be head office staff who handle corporate communications such as annual reports and employee newspapers, while divisional material such as product literature is handled by a local publicity manager, working within corporate disciplines.

Central government and its various departments represent another potentially large client. Their design and publicity requirements are coordinated and handled centrally by the Central Office of Information (COI). Within the COI are a team of communications professionals who deal with specific government departments or handle specialist activities such as audio-visual or exhibitions.

During the mid 1980s, professional bodies such as accountants, solicitors and opticians have changed their attitudes towards publicity, and their members are now allowed to advertise. The professions are a good example of a 'young' prospect group that is gradually moving towards a professional design management system. Initially the contact would have been a senior partner in the practice who initiated and approved the project, and dealt with it on a day-to-day basis. Now marketing and communications specialists are taking on these responsibilities in the larger practices.

Unfortunately, there is no definitive guide to who's who in the communications business. Directories such as the *Advertisers Annual, BRAD Advertiser and Agency List, Willings Press Guide,* and the *Creative Handbook* list major advertisers with the primary contact, but their emphasis is on advertising and public relations rather than design. Articles in the trade magazines – *Campaign, Marketing, Creative Review, Marketing Week, Design and Art Direction,* and *Design Week* – frequently mention the people in client companies who handle advertising accounts. Recruitment advertisements in the same publications and in national newspapers such as the *Guardian* (Creative and Media section) or *The*

Sunday Times may also describe the type of publicity organization within a company. In the absence of published information, you can carry out telephone research to establish your contact. This is likely to give you more accurate and up-to-date information than you might find in a directory, which was probably compiled about a year before publication date. The operator should be able to put you through to the right department, and you can ask who has responsibility for the work that you are interested in.

Contacts for other types of design services

These examples of the contacts for graphic design services illustrate some of the difficulties of identifying and locating the right person. The contacts for other types of design service are otulined in the section on market opportunities. The same research techniques can be used to identify the prospect. As the introduction to this chapter shows, the professional design manager is beginning to play a more prominent role in certain types of design project. Typically they would be found in businesses that placed a great deal of importance on design, and where design had to be integrated with other corporate activities. A design manager could be found in companies using product, retail, packaging or corporate identity design services. In a company that only bought graphic design services, a communications professional would be a more likely prospect.

Refining the prospect list

Marketing any design service is difficult because you have no obvious product to show. What you are offering is the professional expertise to solve a client's problem – in this case communication. Unfortunately not all clients realize the value of professional skills to their business. To demonstrate your expertise you have to rely on examples of work for other people and show how they relate to the current problem. Is your experience relevant and are you really going after the right sort of business?

Desk research on contacts and prospects will indicate the types of company you should be approaching. It is important at an early stage to look at the long-term future of your company. What sort of client list do you want to have? Will they be blue chip clients from any business or do you want to concentrate on one market, and develop a reputation as specialist designers in that field? Do you want to work for a few large companies that will provide a regular flow of work, but within corporate guidelines, or are you the sort of designer who continually needs new challenges. If you need change, perhaps you should be considering a longer list of smaller clients.

Questions like these can help you refine your list of prospects and develop a long-term strategy for building the business you want. The emphasis though is on long term. New business does not appear overnight and you may have to take short-term measures to keep up a minimal workload. If you are successful in getting the right sort of work you may find clients coming to you without any sales effort on your part. Then comes the difficult decision – whether you can handle that work profitably within your overall plans.

Making initial contact

Getting clients is crucial to the successful development of your business, not large numbers of clients – unless you are running a very large organisation – but the types of client who will provide you with a regular flow of work. If your initial research is correct you should now have a list of prime prospects. Converting these to clients is a continuous task.

First you have to make contact so that you can arrange a meeting. Design is a visual commodity. It is difficult to represent it in any other way than by showing examples of your work. There are several ways to make initial contact. The most effective is to prepare an introductory letter or mailing piece outlining your services and experience, and then telephone to ask for an appointment. If your prospect already has a letter, he has some indication of the value of the meeting. A cold telephone call with no prior warning or information can be successful and economical, but it means you have to make a presentation on the telephone without any visual references, and that is a difficult task, even for a tele-sales professional.

The initial mailing carries a lot of responsibility. It has to be a silent salesman for you and create enough interest to make the prospect want to see more of your work. This is no bad discipline; it is no different from what you are trying to achieve for your clients. But companies in the communications business are traditionally bad at their own promotion, so you need to make a conscious effort. The contents of the initial mailing should be simple; they should indicate the type of work you handle, or want to handle for that prospect, your range of services and your experience, and the clients you have already worked for – making sure they are not direct competitors. The more relevant the experience to the prospects' business the better. If you have non-competitive clients in the same business, state that; if you have international campaign experience, and your prospect is a multinational, use that.

Sales letters can be produced very quickly on a computer or word processor, so if you are considering buying one for the business, that is an additional application. You can create a standard letter which you can personalize with the prospect's name. Alternatively, you can merge standard paragraphs, such as lists of clients or details of your services with text aimed specifically at one prospect, for example detailing your experience in that client's market. You can create the mailing list separately and merge it automatically with a choice of letters. You may feel it important to show your prospects examples of your design work straight away – even before your first meeting. Whether you have a specially printed sample to send out or whether you use photographs or other examples depends on the extent of your mailing list. If you are mailing to large numbers of people, printed material is more economical to produce, but if your list is short then you can use photographs or hand-produced materials.

Whatever form your mailing takes it is important that you follow it up quickly. The aim is to arrange a meeting where you can present your work. A telephone call three to four days after the mailing arrives should find your prospect aware of your interest. Telephone sooner and you appear to be rushing things; wait any longer and your prospect will probably have forgotten your letter. For that reason you should not contact too many prospects at the same time. You have to allow time to follow up the mailing, and time to travel to the meeting if your approach is successful. Take on too much and you could lose the initiative in the follow up, or find yourself committed to an embarrassing number of appointments that disrupt your work schedule. Success can bring its own problems.

Generating enquiries

Direct contact is not the only method of reaching prospects – though it can be the most effective. By advertising, issuing press releases or getting listings in a directory you can attract enquiries from people who are actively seeking suppliers. Advertising is effective when it is placed in the right medium. The magazine or newspapers you advertise in should be reaching people who buy design, the people described in the section on contacts. *Marketing* and *Marketing Week* are aimed at the buyers of promotional services, while *Campaign* reaches both buyers and suppliers. *Creative Review, Design and Art Direction, Design Week* and *Design* are written primarily for suppliers in the design and advertising business.

With so much emphasis on media advertising in marketing magazines, design tends to be regarded as a secondary activity, but the magazines do run special features on design and other creative services. Here there is editorial about trends and developments in the design business as well as a listing of suppliers and advertisements placed by suppliers. *British Rate and Data (BRAD)*, a monthly publication, is the best source of information on advertisement rates in these publications, and you can get details of the special features programme direct from the magazine's advertisement department.

Specialized activities like audio-visual, exhibitions and packaging have their own range of publications aimed at people who buy these services. They include *Audio Visual, Packaging Today, Conference World* and *Exhibition Bulletin*. To trace these in *BRAD*, look in the Business Publications classification index. Again the magazines may run special features on design services, but, if not, they normally have a classified section where the main services are listed.

The same magazines form the basis of a press release list. Trade magazines depend on news from people in the industry – news of new products or services, changes in personnel, outstanding achievements, unusual developments or examples of good design. Because most of the magazines have a small editorial staff, they rely on a flow of good press material. Press releases should be factual in tone, rather than promotional. They are not free advertising, but a means of conveying information that is of interest to the whole industry. If you are preparing your own releases, type them double spaced on one side of A4 paper; include a name and address to contact, and indicate whether the information can be published at any time (for immediate release) or whether it is to be held back until a certain date (not for release before ...).

You can also send feature articles to the magazines. They would not be for general release but would be exclusive to one magazine. The length of the article would be 1000 to 2000 words on average and its subject could be an aspect of design that you are expert in. The editors of special features are interested in background articles, such as the basis of good exhibition design, or case histories that help to throw light on longstanding problems such as designing exhibition stands for multiple appearances. If you plan to make press relations an important part of your marketing programme, it could be worth using the services of a public relations consultant or freelance writer. That gives you a professional service and leaves you free to concentrate on design. Writers and public relations consultancies are listed in directories or in publications like *Willings Press Guide*.

Directories could be a useful source of enquiries for your own services. Among the specialized directories of the industry are the *Creative Handbook, Advertisers Annual, Exhibitor's Handbok, ACE Conference Services Directory* and the directory published by *Audio Visual* magazine. If the service you offer is local or regional, rather than national, *Yellow Pages*, the relevant *Thompson Local Directory* or other local guides may be more relevant. Choose your directory carefully. The catch-all heading 'Designers' attracts large numbers of entries, but more specific categories such as 'Designers – packaging' put you into a more specialized market and cut down the competition. You can get details of categories and insertion rates directly from the publications.

Advertising, press relations and directory entries are an alternative to direct contact with your prospect. You should only use them where you believe you have a good chance of generating enquiries. When you get enquiries you need to follow these up quickly, either by sending out further information or by arranging to visit the prospect. If this type of promotion is carried out regularly, you should build up records of useful enquiries as a basis for evaluating the most effective media, and as a guide to future planning.

Professional marketing staff

If the scale of your operations warrants it, you may find it an advantage to use professional marketing staff to build up your business. Some of the larger design consultancies employ full time marketing managers or business development managers to concentrate on new business. This is only a practical proposition if the value of new business that you could handle would cover the costs of the marketing manager. A number of design consultancies employ account handling staff to deal with clients. If they have a background in sales and marketing, they could take on the role of new business development. There are also freelance business development executives who handle sales for a number of clients. They do not normally advertise their services, rather the initiative comes from someone who is seeking to use their services. A typical advertisement would read: 'Expanding consultancy seeks new business partner. Commission on sales. Apply Box Number X.'

The problem with using non-designers for contact with clients and prospects is that the situation is out of your control; it is not you that is presenting your own work, and you lose any opportunity for the personal chemistry that might develop between you and the client. The decision may rest on whether you have the time and the ability to tackle business development successfully without affecting your work for other clients, or whether you would get a greater benefit from using professional marketing people (see Chapter 5, page 79).

Professional marketing staff can be recruited through marketing magazines or through recruitment consultancies specializing in marketing staff.

Presenting your services

When you get the opportunity to meet the prospect, you need to decide on the best method of presenting your services. To show design skills and experience you need to show examples of design work for other people. This could take the form of printed specimens, photographs or models of exhibition stands, and finished photos, and you may also wish to include some of the intermediate or conceptual stages. You can show these in a structured way using a portfolio or slide projector, or you can simply carry around loose samples.

Loose samples rarely survive more than a few presentations in good condition. The constant handling can cause damage. If you are showing examples of illustrations or some other original material, the damage could be extremely expensive. Loose samples can be protected by an encapsulation process which prevents wear, but adds considerably to the weight you have to carry around. The portfolio with clear leaves is a traditional and successful method of presenting visuals, illustrations and finished work. You have a choice of sizes from A3 to A1 – if you can manage that – and various widths to take different quantities of leaves. The portfolio is a flexible presentation medium; you can change the contents to suit the prospect. Each type of presentation would have common elements such as a list of your services, names of your clients and an indication of your main areas of experience. These can be typeset and printed to size.

Another presentation technique is to put your material onto 35mm slide and then show it on a back projection unit. Several companies supply portable desk-top models which come in brief case form, or as a unit with built-in audio recording and playback facilities. All you need is a convenient power point and a surface to put the projector on. Some models come with a conversion lens that allows you to front project onto a remote screen if you have to present to a large group of people. The drawback with slides is that you are relying on mechanical equipment, and no projectors are foolproof. However high your design standards, you can be let down by mechanical failure and that is the part your prospect will remember. The other problem is quality of image. If the photography and processing is correct, the image on the transparency should be good, but if you are projecting in a bright room, much of that quality can be lost. And there is one other subtle loss, your prospect has nothing to pick up and examine.

The content of the presentation should be relevant to the prospect you are meeting. The publications manager of an engineering company will want to know about your experience in dealing with technical literature – how you cope with the detailed product information that is required; a portfolio of consumer advertisements would not be convincing. Similarly, if you are discussing packaging design, examples of exhibition design are no real evidence of your packaging ability. Although you can argue that design skills can be transferred across different media, you are in a competitive market, and the closer the match between your experience and the prospects requirements, the better are your chances.

Demonstrating your professional skills

Marketing design services is not just a matter of presenting work you have done for clients, however relevant it might be. You have to demonstrate that you understand your prospect's requirements and can translate them into viable design services. Marketing design services is primarily a matter of building a prospect's confidence in your professional skills. You can achieve that by demonstrating your ability through case studies – showing the background, markets, proposals and results of a campaign. Research into the nature of your prospect's business can pay dividends – you are aware of the products and the major markets that you will be selling into. You know the information you are looking for, and the briefing session becomes more productive. Briefing sessions are discussed in Chapter 5 on project management. But even at a very early stage where you are meeting a prospect for the first time, you should show that you are a professional.

Following up prospects

The last two sections assumed that you have arranged a preliminary meeting. If that was successful you might have the opportunity to take on a project for a new client – a satisfactory conclusion to a marketing programme. But, if you fail to arrange that initial meeting or if the meeting is open-ended, and your prospect has given you no firm indication that he will be asking you to handle a project, you have to decide what the next stage should be. The first stage is to analyse why the prospect was unwilling to see you. He may be using a supplier who is giving good service and is unwilling to change, or your approach may not have aroused any interest. If that is the case and the prospect is important to your plans, how do you continue from there?

The established supplier situation is the most difficult. Strictly speaking, the designer's professional code of conduct prevents you from approaching the clients of fellow professionals and taking their work away, but this leaves no room for competition. If you believe in your own abilities, you have to convince your prospect that you can handle the business better. As a first step, you need to make sure that the prospect has your name on file, that your name is prominent and that your services are clearly indicated. This is important because established suppliers are not guaranteed work forever; they can make mistakes, and the buyer can change his mind. An established supplier is not a permanent barrier. Although there are no firm rules about the frequency of follow up, you should keep in regular contact without making a nuisance of yourself.

If, on the other hand, your approach has created no interest, you need to look more closely at the sequence of events and the way you presented your services. Was your mailing informative and interesting, was the timing of the telephone follow up right, and did you concentrate on arranging a meeting rather than trying to discuss graphic design over the telephone? Did you carry out your research correctly in the first place? If you find a weak link in the chain, you have to look at the presentation more carefully and make sure every aspect is properly handled. Whatever the problem it is important to keep trying.

You need the same persistance if you are following up a meeting where you had an opportunity to show your work, but were not given the chance to tackle a project straight away. It may simply be a matter of patience; the client might have briefed out his entire promotional programme for the year, and is now unable to start any new projects. The company may only have a small design requirement in which case your research was wrong, or he may be unwilling to take a risk on you. Establishing yourself as a new supplier is often a matter of reducing the risk to your client. If you can demonstrate your ability on small projects, the risk is lower. Produce the results and you are likely to get more work. You don't have to follow up with personal contact; you can carry out follow up mailings, or issue promotional mailings to customers and prospects at regular intervals. This could take the form of give-aways such as wallcharts or desk items, or it could be information on your current facilities and activities, put together as a newsletter.

Monitoring marketing activity

Throughout the marketing process it is important to keep a record of your activities – the successes and the failures. By analysing the results, a pattern should begin to emerge. You can see which industries you are most successful in, what size of company provides the greatest volume of work, how many approaches it took to secure new business, and what ratio of prospects to customers you need to maintain. Monitoring marketing activity helps you continuously to refine and improve your marketing programme.

THREE
Financial Management

Financial management has proved to be the vital spark in design business management. When consultancies go public and appoint professional finance directors, it is a clear sign that management has come of age. Yet, for many designers, finance represents the greatest barrier to their management aspirations. The problem is not confined to design consultancies, however (see Chapter 1, page 4). A survey of professional practices and other small businesses pointed to financial control as the greatest area of weakness; and it took the advertising agency business until 1986 to gain financial respectability in the view of an annual survey conducted by a leading firm of accountants.

Unfortunately, the time when most businesses realize the value of good financial management is when things go wrong – clients pay late or, worse, go bankrupt, suppliers press for settlement of their invoices when there are no funds available, or projects are cancelled, leaving gaping holes in the income forecast.

Financial management is based on knowing what your financial requirements will be, making provision for things that could go wrong, and – most important – knowing the financial state of your business whether it is good or bad. As Michael Peters explained to *Design* magazine, a bad debt from a client left him feeling particularly vulnerable because he did not know his full financial position. He took action quickly though, appointing Bob Silver, a management consultant, to advise him. Silver diagnosed the problem and made recommendations that were designed to keep a tight control on money and ensure that the principals were always fully aware of the practice's financial position. In the modern Michael Peters Group, Bob Silver remains an important figure – but with a different role. He is now responsible for relations with the City and other important financial groups who invest in this public company.

Financial management is a positive tool; it is more than keeping the books and negotiating loans with the bank; it is concerned with the financial implications of decisions about the future of the consultancy. National Westminster Bank, in a leaflet on business finance, pointed out how success and growth can create their own problems. They point to the phenomenon of overtrading, where companies have insufficient funds to meet the higher level of salaries, materials and payments to suppliers that expansion brings.

The decision to put financial management on a proper financial footing is not limited to the large public design groups; medium sized consultancies like Coley, Porter, Bell recognize the contribution of good financial management, and in 1986 appointed a director of finance to strengthen their management team. The freelance or independent designer has financial problems that are different in scale but similar in nature to an established practice. Individuals have to supply information to the Inland Revenue for their assessment, they presumably want to make a profit, and they need to know the extent of their financial commitment. As a freelance, how do you handle your financial affairs and what sort of professional advice is available to you?

This chapter looks at the important elements of financial management in the design business and relates them to the different stages in consultancy development. It is not a comprehensive guide to financial management. Specialist books (listed in the reference section) will provide a fuller explanation.

Financial management is essentially about balancing income and expenditure, and controlling costs to achieve a profit. If you make a profit you are liable to pay a number of different taxes on it. This sets the scene for the responsibilities of a financial manager – recording and controlling the elements of income and expenditure to improve profitability and reduce taxation. The financial manager has access to different sources of funds to balance the gap between income and expenditure, and uses a variety of management tools to help control finance and assess the performance of the business.

All designers, whatever their scale of operation, are concerned with the level of fees they earn. Income is therefore the first element of the financial equation. Given the nature of the design business, operating on ad hoc projects rather than on a forecast income, the fee level is critical; but what should that be? In the absence of a published scale of professional fees, designers have to make individual decisions about the fees they charge. The Design Council recommended a maximum daily rate of £300 in 1986 for participants in the Support for Design scheme, but as one correspondent pointed out this would prove unprofitable for large consultancies and very lucrative for smaller ones. The level of fee should in theory relate to the cost structure of the consultancy; that is the traditional starting point for calculating the fee level, but, in a competitive marketplace, this can count for little. Most consultancies can quote horror stories about a realistic estimate they put in for a project, only to find themselves undercut by a ridiculous amount. The question of fees and speculative pitching receives regular attention in the press and is a particular concern of the Design Business Group.

The question of fee levels reflects the current debate over professionalism and commercialism in design. Unfortunately, because of the diverse nature of design projects, a simple scale of fees – like that published by other professions – seems an unlikely prospect. *Design Week* magazine has made a useful contribution to business understanding by publishing the fees for a project wherever possible; but, given the natural reluctance to disclose confidential information and the occasional storm of controversy that surrounds published figures, this is unlikely to produce a definitive guide to fees. What is often missing from a news item is any detail on what the fee covered. Following one report in the magazine on a corporate identity programme for a printer, there was strong comment from another design group on the time scale and level of charges for the project. The issue was finally resolved when the design consultants replied that the project fee quoted in the article included the time and cost of the implementation of the programme, and that their fee represented only a small proportion of the total charge.

In calculating fees, the scale of the project and its commercial implications has to be carefully considered. The traditional method of ad hoc fees for design projects may not always be the most satisfactory or the most profitable. A recent trend in product design, for example, is to charge a basic fee for the initial design work and take a subsequent royalty income from sales of the finished product. This gives an additional commercial incentive to the designer. The work of retail specialists, Piper (discussed in Chapter 6 on expansion), shows how designers can take a positive lead in this by developing their own product, taking part in joint ventures and even opening their own retail outlets. Designers and clients who work together on a number of different projects are also realizing the benefits of payment by retainer.

The second element of design finance is cost – how much does it cost to run the business? Though it may seem difficult to understand the nature of costing, this can make the greatest contribution to financial improvement. An item by item checklist is sometimes the only way to be sure that all costs have been included in a forecast. Cost control can be a time-consuming process but it repays the attention to detail. In industry, the drive for cost reduction is a continuous process, but little is published about the process in design. The most prominent examples were the series of redundancies in Fitch, McColl and AID in the late 1980s, but these were prompted by a down turn in work and a reduction of staff to match the lower level of business. With the development of professional design management, cost control could become a more important exercise.

Putting costs and income together gives the first equation in financial management: if income is greater then cost you are running a profitable business; but, if the trend is continuously in the opposite direction, you need help. Profitability is at the heart of the business system; it is not a method of exploiting your employees or your clients, it is simply an expression of the financial soundness of the business. Profit is not a sum of money that goes into the pockets of the partners; in many cases it is only a figure on paper and is often used to finance other developments in the business. Profit can be expressed in a number of ways and this gives you a basis for comparing your performance with others in the same market. Total profit shows how much money you are making, but is no basis for comparing large and small, or efficient and inefficient companies. Profit can also be expressed as a percentage of your turnover; this shows that you might be handling a lot of business, but if it is not profitable it could be the wrong sort of business – work that is very time consuming, or work that has been charged at too low a rate.

When the business is growing, profitability becomes an important indicator of progress. In the mid 1980s a number of medium sized design groups joined larger communications groups; the designers who joined the groups commented that professional financial control and access to group funds were, for them, the major benefits of the merger. As part of the group management process, the designers had to set annual profit targets and all other financial targets were built around those. Profitability becomes an important business target for consultancies that have gone public. The owners of the company are the shareholders and they are advised by analysts; both demand continuous high performance to earn a return on their investment. If there are no profits, the company is unlikely to have any shareholders, and the company loses access to the funds it needs to sustain its high level of activity and expansion.

Building up the level of profitable business and reducing the level of tax paid on that profit are two of the main responsibilities of the finance manager. The traditional concept of the finance manager was of a book-keeper – someone who recorded what had happened in the business. This remains an essential function – and for many smaller businesses, the only function – that is needed. But the finance manager plays a more positive role when he looks forwards as well as backwards. This forward looking role is important when a consultancy is growing – working to three or five year plans. The growth plans cover marketing objectives, forecasts of turnover, staff levels and investment in premises and equipment that will sustain growth. The financial forecasts need justification and a careful level of planning to avoid the problem of overtrading.

Who is to handle financial management when it gets to this level of sophistication? The trend in large and medium sized groups is to appoint professional finance managers from industry, but they may not be familiar with the special requirements of the design industry – ad hoc projects, long lead times and a difficult costing base. Finance managers who have come through the design business are certainly familiar with design and its special problems, but they may not have the depth of financial skills to match the professionals.

Income of a design business

Design fees

A designer's main source of income is fees for design services. The client is charged a total fee for the project based on the hourly rate established by the designer multiplied by the number of hours spent on the project. Alternatively, the fee can be based on the estimated value of the project to the client. In the absence of a scale of professional fees, the fee level is set by the designer. Design fees cover design and consultation with the client. Other services that form part of a project are covered by a management fee, described in the next section. The fee should cover all the services that could be provided during a project, as shown in Chapter 5, page 86.

Fees are paid at the end of a project, or at the end of an agreed stage on a long project. Annual fee income is therefore based on the number of projects or stages completed during the designer's financial year. If a project is abandoned, the client should pay costs to date. A client should also pay for design proposals where these form part of a pitch for the business.

Management fees

A management fee is a charge for providing services other than design. These could include supervising subcontractors or suppliers – photographers, shopfitters, printers, illustrators – or buying in other services or materials on behalf of the client – a set of slides or an exhibition stand, for example. The management fee covers two main costs to the designer – the time spent in providing the service and the cost of financing any purchases. Examples are given on page 86 of Chapter 5 on project management. The production stage of a brochure, for example, could involve selecting a shortlist of printers, reviewing estimates, choosing and briefing a supplier, checking proofs, arranging delivery and administering the production process.

The second element – financing the purchase – is necessary because there could be a time lag between the designer paying the supplier and the client paying the designer. The cost is equivalent to the interest payed on money borrowed to pay the supplier.

There are two ways to calculate a management fee:

- Estimating the time and cost factors and charging at the hourly rate.
- Adding a percentage to the cost of any bought-in services; typical figures could be fifteen to twenty-five per cent of the supplier's invoice. The percentage should cover your costs and allow a margin of profit.

Royalty income

In product design, the payment of royalties to designers has added a commercial incentive to the design process. A royalty is a payment, normally a percentage of the selling price, for each product sold. The royalty rate would be agreed between client and designer and should be confirmed in a contract. The total royalty payment is calculated on the basis of sales figures supplied by the client. The introduction of royalties has led to a number of different arrangements for product design remuneration:

- Fee only
- Royalty only
- Combined fee and royalty.

A variation of the royalty agreement is the joint venture where designer and client share the commercial risks and costs in developing a product and, in return, take an agreed share of the profit or income. Here the designer receives only a royalty; his contribution is the design. A number of design practices are also developing their own products and licencing them for manufacture (see Chapter 6, page 96).

Retainers

Design fees, royalty income and management fees are sources of income related to individual projects. Forecasting annual project income is difficult and in contrast to the situation of an advertising agency or public relations consultancy where the client allocates an annual budget to support a product. The retainer is one form of income which can add more stability. The client pays on agreed sum to cover a year's service; the designer provides a specified number of hours' design and consultancy services, but would charge bought-in costs extra. The fee is invoiced regularly, say monthly or quarterly.

Retainers provide continuity for both designer and client, but should be planned and controlled carefully so that they represent value for money and profitable business. A retainer which puts a premium on the designer's skills, but does not involve excessive design time, represents profitable business; however, an account where the client tries to get the maximum amount of design work for the minimum retainer may provide continuity but could prove unprofitable.

Fees for consultancy

Some clients may only need a consultancy service – using the designer's expertise to provide preliminary advice and recommendations, but carrying out detailed design work and implementation through other sources. An example is a feasibility study for a new corporate identity scheme or a packaging redesign. A designer can also oversee the work of other suppliers, managing a print programme, for example, or acting as a quality controller over other design consultancies. The fee for this is an ad hoc charge based on the cost of the designer's involvement, or it can form part of a design retainer.

Calculating hourly rates

The hourly rate affects all your pricing decisions – the rate you quote a client, the project estimate, the final invoice and the analysis of the time you spend on a project. Many factors should be considered in calculating the hourly rate:

- Your own costs for providing the service
- The income you want to earn
- Competitive rates
- The value of the project to the client.

The starting point is overheads (calculating these is discussed in the section on design costs – see page 48). Take the total overheads for the year, divide them into a convenient unit such as a week or a month and then divide the figure again by the number of working hours. That gives the basic cost for a working hour. Add a percentage to that for profit and reserves to give a basic hourly rate. Look at the forecasts for workload to see how many chargeable hours it adds up to. If the workload is low the income from a low hourly rate may not be sufficient to meet the income target. You also have to make marketing decisions about the rate; how would it work in the context of a long job; how does it compare with competitive rates; and would it represent value for money to your client?

Chargeable costs

In costing a project, look very carefully at all the elements that could be included. Design time and production costs are the basic elements, but there are many other areas of cost. Take exhibition design as an example. A great deal of time will be spent on meetings with clients and suppliers, briefing and checking progress and quality, ordering materials and carrying out general administration. These are all time consuming activities and should be charged. Each project will vary but you should compile a checklist to help you include all cost elements – see page 86 in Chapter 5 on project management for examples. Some of these time-based services would be charged at the full hourly rate, but travel or services that could be carried out by administrative staff or junior designers would normally be charged at a reduced rate.

Competitive pricing

In the absence of any professional guidelines designers set their own fee levels. Although it is professional practice not to undercut other designers, there is still competition in the marketplace and the designer must take that into account. Price is rarely the most important factor in selecting a design group, but clients do consider it. In a simple project a freelance designer with low overheads would be more economical than a large practice, but in a complex project with tight deadlines the freelance designer's price advantage might be worthless because of the resources needed to complete the project on time.

However, in a competitive situation, the larger consultancy is generally at a price disadvantage. If it needs the work, a decision has to be made on differential pricing – taking a reduced profit on the job, splitting the project between senior and junior designers, getting improved production estimates from suppliers and subcontractors, or offering the client a reduced level of service (see Chapter 2, page 23).

Estimating

An estimate can only be as accurate as the brief a designer is given. Before the start of a project, detailed information is likely to be minimal so estimating usually proceeds in stages. A first stage estimate covers the cost of preparing initial design proposals either in the form of a report or as finished visuals. This estimate should include a calculation of the design fee and would include any other chargeable cost elements that have been identified. When the proposals have been accepted and approved, it is possible to prepare a project specification that includes detailed design and production costs. The final estimate is built up from forecasts of your own time for design and administration, and quotations from suppliers together with a management fee based on the supplier's charges. Even at this stage, there may be undefined areas, so the estimate should contain a reserve to cover uncertainties. An estimate is not a binding document although clients prefer a degree of certainty; it should state that the prices are at today's costs which covers you against price rises from your suppliers.

Overspends

Estimates are essentially forecasts of expenditure on a project, they cannot take account of changes or other unforeseen problems. Financial control is good professional practice, so you should aim to eliminate as many uncertainties as possible. Author's corrections cannot be predicted and these should be charged extra; in a brochure this could include changes to an approved text or a change of illustration subject; in product design a late change to specification. The charges for work additional to budget are more difficult to allocate. If the job takes longer than you had estimated, the client would argue that you should be more accurate in your estimating, but if the extra work was caused by a poor brief or a difficult client, the onus is on you to prove that the additional costs are justified. You should always itemize these additional costs when you submit an invoice.

Costs of a design business

Design costs – an overview

Monitoring costs is one of the most important responsibilities of financial management. The first stage is to identify your cost structure which varies with the size of the practice, the workload and the stage the business has reached. The cost structure for a freelance is different from that of a large practice, while a practice that is just setting up or expanding repaidly will incur costs that do not apply to an established business. It is important to recognize these distinctions because some costs may not recur in another financial year and can distort your forecasts. A strong marketing drive, for example, can add costs, while a short-term change in the level of work can influence costs and cash requirements in different ways. The remainder of this section explains those differences and helps designers identify their own cost structure.

Running costs

Running costs include all those elements that are necessary to keep the practice operating; they are independent of project costs. A checklist should help you to identify your own running costs. The following list is not comprehensive, but represents the costs incurred by most design practices:

- Rent
- Rates
- Heating
- Lighting
- Gas
- Electricity
- Cleaning
- Maintenance
- Telephone
- Stationery
- Insurance
- Accountancy
- Materials
- Furniture
- Equipment.

Project costs

Project costs are of two kinds, those that are chargeable to your client and those that include the cost of running that particular project. The section on chargeable costs describe the elements that could be charged directly to a client. Indirect costs cover the management of that project – the costs to you of handling the project – and include administration and the costs of financing the project.

Staff costs

Staff costs account for the highest proportion of design costs, whether it is a freelance business or a large practice. An individual self-employed designer has to pay himself a wage and cover national insurance contributions as well as personal accident insurance, pension contributions and other forms of insurance. When you employ staff, you incur the same costs for each member of staff together with:

• Costs of administering tax and other personal legislation.
• Providing staff resources, holiday pay, statutory sick pay, canteen facilities or luncheon vouchers.
• Staff training.
• Staff incentives including bonuses, company cars, share ownership schemes, travel subsidies.
• Recruitment costs including advertising, payments to recruitment agencies or headhunters.

Chapter 4 on personnel management describes these in more detail.

Start-up costs

A design business could be run on a minimal budget – a drawing board set up in a spare room at home. This is unlikely to remain a satisfactory solution; the designer or the new practice has to find premises, equip them and set up the business. Additional costs in the first year of the new business could include:

• Buying or renting premises
• Legal fees
• Removal expenses
• Business registration
• Production of stationery
• Building, decorating or conversion work.

Replacement costs

When equipment wears out it has to be replaced. Cost forecasts should take account of the designed life of expensive equipment and its likely date of replacement. Replacement is not just a matter of renewing equipment that has worn out. If you use facsimile, computer-aided design, word processors or other high technology equipment it is important to keep up to date with technological change to retain a competitive advantage.

Expansion costs

Business growth is not always planned and it is difficult to predict the changes in cost structure. The changes begin with an increase in overtime payments or salaries of additional staff to handle the increased workload. The greater level of payment to suppliers and subcontractors that have to be financed can create cashflow problems. Planned expansion introduces a whole range of other costs which are discussed in Chapter 6 on expansion.

Marketing costs

Marketing costs are ad hoc costs which include the costs of occasional campaigns and regular advertising. There are direct and indirect costs: direct costs include advertising space and production, production of mail shots and postage, and the costs of employing marketing specialists; indirect costs cover your own time in preparing promotional material, following up mail shots and visiting prospects. Marketing costs are usually compared with the results they achieve and in that sense, marketing is an investment cost (see Chapter 2, page 40).

Overheads and variable costs

Overheads is a term that is applied to running costs that cannot be avoided. Whatever level of work you are handling, overheads remain constant. Variable costs, as the name suggests are those that vary with the level of work.

Books on small business finance (listed in the reference section) can give you more information on costs and the calculation of charges.

Financial management

Introduction

The responsibilities of a financial manager are to:

- Maintain records.
- Manage the tax affairs of the company.
- Ensure that the company has adequate sources of funds.
- Ensure that the company makes a suitable level of profit.
- Supply management information so that everyone is aware of the financial state of the company.
- Advise on the financial implications of any decisions that are made.
- Advise on the funds that will be needed to maintain certain levels of work.
- Handle financial relations, particularly in public consultancies.

Financial staff

The level of financial management grows more sophisticated as the size and complexity of the consultancy grows. The small practice would need someone with basic accounting skills to handle the bookkeeping functions, while decision-making would remain in the hands of the partners. A management accountant would be needed at the next stage – when the consultancy employed more than thirty people and had a turnover, of, say, £5 million. The accountant would play a management role in the company, acting as company secretary, for example dealing with legal and business matters as well as financial affairs. The management accountant would take on more of an advisory role, providing financial information and advice to the decision-makers. A large consultancy, with a turnover of more than £10 million, would need a financial manager with considerable professional experience. When the finance manager reaches that level of seniority, he becomes involved in general policy-making decisions, as well as taking responsibility for all financial decisions.

Recruiting financial staff with relevant experience can be difficult; you will be looking for professional skills and qualifications at the right management level, but far more important is the right sort of experience. Design finance has special needs – meeting the costs of high staff levels, low investment and a cash flow affected by a large number of individual projects. The ideal candidate would have experience in a related field. (See Chapter 4 on page 70).

The professional institutes, such as the Chartered Institute of Management Accountants or the Institute of Chartered Accountants, can give you information on the qualifications of their members. Recruitment consultants, specializing in accountancy staff or senior finance executives can help you locate the right candidates.

Financial planning

Financial planning is concerned with the short- and long-term cash requirements of the business. In the short term, it concentrates on the forecast of income and expenditure for the current year. It highlights any shortfalls in funding or in the level of work to generate planned income. This can influence the requirements for borrowing and for developing a stronger marketing effort. In the longer term it considers future income and expenditure for a number of planned levels of activity – marketing costs to reach the planned level of business, staff costs to handle that level of activity, changes in the requirements for funds to finance new levels of work in progress. Expansion could also require a change of premises or investment in new equipment to improve efficiency.

Management information

Management information forms the basis of effective decision-making. A formal management report would include the value of work in progress – projects not yet completed that will generate future income – with an indication of when the work will be completed; the amount of work that has been invoiced or paid in the month; and the credit control situation – which clients are paying on time and which are slow. The report would also include information on the company's progress in the year to date – turnover, sales by client, cash flow, profit to date and bank balances.

Computer-based systems, which process information quickly, provide an excellent method for reporting (see Chapter 4, page 71). Presentation of the information should be clear so that everyone knows the implications and action required. The report should not just be a matter of record, it should be a basis for action – corrective action if necessary to increase the level of work and income, or to improve cash flow. The reports should be compiled at least once a month, but in a more volatile situation or in a fast moving business, weekly statements may be more useful.

Financial relations

Financial information is not only important to the consultancy, it can affect the practice's relations with customers and other influential groups. Customers want to know that the practice is financially stable – that it will not go down in the middle of a vital project. They may be happier dealing with a successful consultancy, though not one that is profiting at its expense. Banks and financial institutions are also important targets; in making decisions on support and finance, they need to be aware of the current financial situation and the prospects of the people who want to borrow. A strong financial relations programme is essential for practices who are going public or who are thinking of doing so. The investors who are considering where to put their money need to be constantly updated on potential and performance. Where the number of people who need to know is small, direct mail of annual and quarterly results would be sufficient, but in a public company the information flow must be constant. Financial relations here forms a distinct branch of public relations and the efforts to keep shareholders informed could include:

- Regular press releases on financial performance, business development and management.
- Feature articles on business development in financial management and investment journals.
- Publication of financial information through interim or annual reports.
- Presentations to investors and stockbroker briefings.

Chapter 2 on marketing explains presentation and press information techniques. If your expansion programme makes financial relations essential, consider using a public relations consultancy specializing in investor or financial relations.

Financial management and decision making

Earlier sections discussed the financial implications of decision-making. The financial manager's role is to look at the cost and revenue elements of any particular decision and to advise on the most effective solution. In that way, he can help to evaluate alternative strategies. In a marketing programme, for example, he could advise on the cost-effectiveness of different levels of marketing support. Relocating too is a decision with financial implications; moving to new premises could improve the efficiency of the company, but the move could affect the cost structure of the company and destroy any other advantages.

Public consultancies

When a consultancy goes public it takes on certain financial responsibilities that do not apply to other design consultancies. The reason for going public is to raise additional sources of finance; this money comes from investors who exchange their money for shares which they expect to increase in value and which pay them a good dividend. The onus is therefore on the consultancy to produce good performances to generate profits. There are additional responsibilities that are outside the scope of this book and require professional advice.

A consultancy that has reached a position where it is considering going public will probably be using financial advisers. One of the large accountancy firms can provide flotation advice and act as reporting accountants. They and the Stock Exchange publish guides to flotation. (See Chapter 6, page 98).

Budgets

Budgets are the basis of financial planning and control. They are established for periods of a month or a year and lay down the guideliness for target levels of income and expenditure. Budgets are derived from the overall financial plan and break it down into individual targets so that specific areas of cost and income can be identified and controlled more easily. A monthly expenditure budget, for example, shows any forthcoming expenditure that might need attention. Budgeting helps to keep everyone aware of what they should be achieving.

Operating statements

Operating statements are the most common form of management information. They are associated with budgets, and report on the financial state of the company, showing how the consultancy is performing against budget together with many other aspects of performance. The operating statement is a record of financial achievement and monitors progress; it includes updated information on work in progress, cash requirements and contribution to profit.

Recording systems

The basis of any management information tool is an effective recording system. This is a method of capturing information quickly and making it available for analysis and reporting. Traditional methods are based on manual operations and need clerical staff to create one set of records and modify it for management reporting.

The time sheet was the basis of the system, and it still works in the smaller practice; the time sheet has divisions for different days, hours and parts of an hour; it is split by project so that time can be allocated to the right place. Anyone who is working on a project fills in chargeable time under that number, and at the end of a week or month the time is collected and held in a job file. Any other costs related to the project are collected in the same file. The easiest way to control these other costs is to issue an order for any purchase, and give the supplier the job number so that the information gets to the right place. (Examples of a time sheet are illustrated in Figs. 5.1 and 5.2 in Chapter 5 – see pp. 90–1.)

The time sheet and job file method works well enough where the number of designers and projects is small; however, the information needs further processing before it is suitable for reporting and analysis and there could be a delay. In a large practice, where the project flow is more complex and there are more designers, delay could be costly. A computer-based recording system offers considerably more flexibility; the systems and the facilities are described in more detail in Chapters 4 and 5 on personnel and project management. Here the designer and other people key the information in at a terminal. A software program processes the information and adds it to any other cost information that is already there. The information is always up to date and it can be processed immediately for reporting and analysis.

The section on new technology on pages 70–4 in Chapter 4 describes how computers can be applied to the design business. For more information on computers and recording software, check the manufacturers' literature or ask the advice of a computer consultant.

Cost-benefit analysis

A purchase decision is rarely straightforward. There is likely to be a choice of competing products, and in the absence of unlimited funds, decisions have to be made on the priority of purchases. In that situation how do you decide on the importance of purchases? A technique known as cost-benefit analysis provides a degree of support; here the costs of a purchase are compared with its potential benefit. Ideally the benefit should be one that can be quantified in some way – reduced costs or increased income. The example below showing the decisions behind purchase of a facsimile (fax) machine illustrates the principles of cost-benefit analysis.

Annual cost of buying or leasing fax machine	£a
Annual running costs of fax	£b
Annual cost of sending messengers to main fax destinations	£c
Cost of other potential applications	£d
Potential annual savings from using fax	£e

This financial analysis does not include any estimate of the business benefits of using fax. These are harder to quantify.

Profitability analysis

The aim of financial management is to ensure that the consultancy is making a worthwhile profit on the work it is producing. Overall profit is important – assessing the consultancy's performance at the end of the financial year – but it is equally important to analyse the profitability of individual accounts to see the level of contribution they are making. An account can be very important in terms of turnover, but, if it makes very little profit contribution, it may not be so valuable. This type of information would not be obvious in an overall analysis. Profitability analysis is a useful way of comparing different accounts:

Client	Turnover	Profit	Percentage Profit
Smith Stores	£100,000	£10,000	10
Bright Packaging	£250,000	£20,000	8
Power Products	£75,000	£15,000	20

An account may need corrective action if it is not profitable, looking at factors such as pricing, level of service, type of work, or working methods with the client.

Comparative performance

Your practice may be doing well on its own terms but it can be valuable to compare performance with the rest of the design business. In 1987 there was no comprehensive information available on the financial performance of design, but *Design Week* had made a start with its survey of fees and staffing levels.

A related example of comparative performance for the advertising business is *Campaign* magazine's annual league table of agency performance in different areas.

Sources of funds

Introduction

Balancing income and expenditure is an important objective of financial management, but there are times when additional funds will be needed. Trying to get access to cash when you most need it can prove difficult, so it is easier to forecast your funding requirements in advance. Funding is a long- and short-term technique. Short-term funding helps you get over temporary cash flow problems or make smaller purchases; long-term finance is to cover larger purchases or is used for a programme of expansion. The first stage is to consider why the funding is required; the second to analyse the cause of the shortfall. The problem may need remedial action rather than borrowing. A shortage of cash, for example, can be caused by poor credit control – tighter controls, a change of payment terms or the use of factoring facilities could improve that. In this section we look at different ways of generating money from the business or raising funds outside.

Credit control

The term credit refers to the payment terms you offer your customers – a credit period of, say, thirty days to settle your invoice. The problem with any business is that customers don't want to pay what they owe. Customers are invariably late in paying and some don't want to pay at all. As a first stage, always manage payment administration efficiently; clear invoices delivered quickly after the job with terms of payment clearly stated should help you get payment when it is due. Statements are the next stage; they remind the client that their terms of payment have been exceeded and that payment is now due.

At the end of the payment period, you can take a number of different courses of action. Written reminders and telephone calls to the accounts department are the starting point. If there is still no response you can threaten legal action, putting the matter in the hands of your solicitor and asking for settlement within the normal terms of your business. If there is still no response, you have the option of going ahead with legal action, which can be expensive. However, there is an alternative if your claim for settlement is under a certain value, currently approximately £500. The Small Claims Court can handle disputes of this sort for a fixed fee; provided the claim is a genuine one you should recover your money.

Credit control is about keeping close control on whether your clients are paying or not paying, and reducing the outstanding debt to a minimum. An alternative is to use a factoring service to receive quick settlement of your invoices. The factoring company buys your invoices and collects them, charging you a percentage of the invoice as a service fee and paying the balance immediately. The result is that you get a much improved cash flow, while the potential interest you would have to pay is probably less than the charges for the service. The other advantage is that the factors check out the creditworthiness of your clients and this helps to improve reliability.

Factoring services are offered by the major banks and are advertised in business and management magazines.

Alternative funding

An alternative method of paying for supplies and equipment can help to release funds. Using loans in preference to cash can leave the cash free for other purposes. Leasing and lease purchase is an increasingly popular form of acquiring equipment that you don't have to own. Here you make a regular payment to the leasing company and in return you have the use of the asset without physically owning it. Purchase leaseback is an extension of this where you originally buy the equipment and then assign it to a leasing company who lend you an equivalent sum of money; with your repayments you lease the product. If you own your premises you can raise money by mortgaging your property. This can provide useful security for a large loan. The point of alternative funding is not to take out new loans, but to rearrange the financing of your existing assets so that you have more cash available.

Alternative funding can be arranged through banks or finance companies. An accountant can advise you on the most suitable arrangements.

Raising capital

Major expenditure or the resources to expand, move to new premises, take on new staff or start an acquisition programme creates a demand for additional capital. One way is by issuing shares in the consultancy. In return for money, the shareholder receives an allocation and gains partial ownership of the consultancy. Share ownership can be private or public; in private ownership the shares remain within the consultancy – its directors, employees and their families. Public ownership means that anyone can buy the shares which are sold through a recognized financial institution.

The most common pattern is for the founders or senior managers of a consultancy to put money into the company and become shareholding directors. There is a limit to the number of potential shareholding directors to be found in a consultancy and to the amount of money they can raise. Outside sources of finance therefore become more critical at a certain stage in the company's growth. However, there is a considerable difference in attitude between private and public shareholders. Private shareholders see shares as an incentive or a reward for effort; public shareholders, however, are looking for an investment that will give them a good return; they have no responsibility for the business.

The mechanics of share ownership are that the shareholder pays a sum of money and receives certificates; they also receive an annual dividend which is based on the number of shares they hold and the company's performance. An accountant and a solicitor can advise on the proper procedures for share issue.

Increasing income

One reason for seeking additional funding is that income and expenditure are out of balance. The simplest solution is to increase income, but a higher work level adds to costs, so the aim should be to increase income without adding too much to costs. This can be achieved by getting more business to increase turnover but handling the new work with the same resources – a higher workload on the same number of staff. Your overheads are not increased. Putting up your charges can also increase income without adding to costs. You should also consider other ways of earning income – asking for royalties on sales, rather than a design fee, for example, if the product you have designed is selling in high volume.

Overdrafts

Overdrafts are one of the simplest and cheapest forms of borrowing. They are designed to meet short-term cash requirements – when you are waiting for settlement or when you are being pressed for payment. A bank can make an overdraft arrangement with you for payments up to a certain level. The overdraft is settled when it is repaid, and you are charged interest on a quarterly basis on the amount outstanding. The advantage of an overdraft is that it is flexible and is only used when it is needed. If you need extra funds to make a major purchase or if you have a permanent cash shortage you should consider other methods of funding.

Loans

Unlike an overdraft, a loan is taken out for a specific purpose – either to finance a particular purchase or as part of an expansion programme. The variety of loans, their terms and their sources are changing rapidly and are too numerous to describe, but they fall into three main categories – short-, medium- and long-term. Term refers to the number of years available to pay the loan; the term you choose depends on the size of the loan, your ability to meet a certain level of repayments and the useful life of the equipment you are buying. For example, it would be impractical to take out a ten year loan on a piece of studio equipment that only had a useful life of five years; the repayments might be smaller, but the overall cost is likely to be higher when you add ten years' interest, and – for the later part of the term – you will be paying for something that is no longer useful to you.

The sources for loans have multiplied since deregulation of the financial institutions: the list now includes clearing banks, building societies, insurance companies, merchant banks and other institutions. In looking at the loan services available you should consider the terms, rate of interest, security requirements and any other special conditions imposed by the lender.

An accountant can advise you on the type of loan that is most suitable for your purpose.

Grants and subsidies

The government has developed a number of small business schemes to help people start up. Examples include enterprise zone schemes for those starting up in areas of high unemployment and grants for small workshop operations in rural areas. There are also grants for the recently unemployed to help start up businesses; one such scheme guarantees a minimum weekly wage for the first year of the business.

Cost reduction

The second move is to reduce costs wherever possible; this is a well-tried method in industry where there are many areas of potential reduction; but in design, and in the professions generally, skilled staff are the largest cost element and the most important part of the business. Cost reduction should not lead to a reduction in the level of service; this could be detrimental to the business in the long term. There are other areas of potential cost reduction – looking at overheads, buying more efficiently from suppliers, or, if it really is necessary, cutting down the level of service. It is a dangerous move to cut down on investment expenditure because this can affect the long-term prospects of the business.

Fund proposals

When you are raising funds, you have to convince the lender that you are going to make sensible use of the funds, that you are in a position to repay the loan and that the lender will benefit financially from his involvement. The major clearing banks produce documents showing how to construct a funding proposal. These contain all the information the lender needs to know and form a useful checklist.

Profit and loss

Balancing income and expenditure

The first stage of financial management is to balance income and expenditure and to aim at an excess of income. Annual income depends on the volume of work going through the consultancy and speed of settlement by your clients. You have to make sure that the planned level of income for the year is sufficient to cover your overheads, and the variable costs that arise on individual projects. Your invoicing forecasts should cover the full period of a year, but if projects finish outside the period they cannot be counted as part of annual income. Expenditure should be forecast for the same period.

Cash flow

Cash flow is one of the critical factors in business finance; it refers to the timing and availability of cash and its relation to essential expenditure. Income and expenditure are only figures on paper; until you actually receive payment and settle your debts they are meaningless. Your cash flow plan should show when you expect to receive the money – making allowances for normal terms of credit – and when you have to pay it out, again making allowance for normal credit terms. You can then refine your forecast by looking at the possibility of invoicing in stages, tightening credit terms or extending credit with your suppliers. The gaps in your cash flow projections have to be covered by additional funding. The section on funding shows how to achieve this – see pages 55–8.

Profitability

The aim of any business is to make a profit – that is an excess of income over expenditure. Profit is needed to provide further funds for expansion, to provide a reward in the form of a dividend to people who have put money into the business – either the founders or the shareholders – to provide a basis for taxation, and to measure the efficiency of the business. Profit is measured by deducting your total annual expenditure from your total annual income. This gives you the basic profit before tax. Other forms of expenditure such as capital expenditure can be deducted to give you a pre-tax profit, while net profit represents the profit remaining after tax.

Taxation

Personal income tax

Whether you work as an individual or employ other people, you are responsible for the payment of personal income tax. This is based on individual's earnings – his wages plus any bonuses or benefits he receives from employment. Against this are set the various forms of personal allowance to calculate the individual's personal liability to tax. Tax rates vary from year to year and you can get current information from the tax office. An employee's income tax is collected regularly at source – deducted from weekly or monthly pay packets – but a self-employed person has to submit annual accounts that show income and expenditure for the year. The self-employed person's income tax is calculated annually but paid in arrears.

Tax on profits

As well as the tax that the individuals in a practice pay, the practice has to pay a tax on profits. The tax is assessed on the profit during a full financial year and is normally paid a year in arrears. A company's financial year can start on any date, although some are more convenient than others. As we showed in an earlier section, profits are calculate by deducting expenditure from income. However, to calculate the taxable profit, the expenditure must be allowable. The Inland Revenue or your accountant can advise you on the type of expenditure that is allowable.

Value-added tax

VAT is a tax that is added to the selling price of goods or services that you supply to your customers. The current rate of VAT is fifteen per cent and it is levied when your annual turnover exceeds a certain level. VAT is not a charge that you benefit from, you have to collect it from your customers and then return it to the VAT collectors. VAT is also levied on goods and services that you buy but you can claim the tax back from the collector. In preparing your own income and expenditure forecasts you should not take VAT into account. Not all services carry VAT – printed items, for example, are zero rated, but components of a printed job such as design, typesetting or photography do carry VAT if they are supplied separately. The VAT office can advise you on their requirements. VAT administration requires strict record keeping and you have to make regular returns to the inspectors. VAT is normally paid quarterly and there are penalties for avoiding it.

Capital taxes

Capital gains and capital allowances are closely linked. Capital expenditure is a term used to describe the purchase of large or valuable equipment such as vehicles, computers and buildings. You can claim capital allowances on items like these to cover what is called depreciation. Depreciation is an accounting term which describes a loss of value over a period of time. These capital allowances can be set against your taxable income to reduce your tax bill but, if you sell the item you have claimed allowances on, that is called a capital gain. Tax is charged on that gain separately.

A tax inspector or your accountant can advise you on your liability for capital taxes.

Tax records

To ensure that all your dealings with the tax authorities are straightforward, you have to keep good records. For the self-employed person that means keeping details of all income, full records of all deductible expenditure, and keeping receipts of all payments. Limited companies have their accounts professionally audited so that they are acceptable to the Inland Revenue.

Tax losses

Despite your efforts to build a profitable business, you can make a tax loss during a financial year if your expenditure is greater than your income. Tax losses are treated by the Inland Revenue as deductible items which can be set against future profits.

Financial records

Purchase records

Purchase records are sometimes referred to in accounting terms as the bought ledger; it is a record of all the purchases in the company. It shows the source of the purchase, its value, any VAT content, the invoice details and the date of payment. This is basic costing information, but it can also be used in business analysis. The costs should be allocated to individual clients or projects and these can be analysed to show the levels and efficiency of purchasing. Volume purchasing can qualify for valuable discounts, so it is worth analysing your purchasing patterns to see if they can be improved.

Sales records

Sales records are recorded on a client-by-client basis and show each purchase with its value, starting date, date of invoice and payment. Sales records help to build up a profile of your business to see what clients are buying, what their purchasing level is, and their frequency of purchase. This information gives you a basis for forecasting and analysis.

Annual reports

Annual reports are a legal requirement for consultancies who have gone public and who have to provide information on their performance to shareholders. The core of an annual report is the accounting section which shows turnover, profit and loss and other figures, but the report also contains a review of activities. If there have been acquisitions or any other form of diversification, there should be a description of how it fits into the group structure and what prospects it offers the company. Although the annual report is a compulsory document for public consultancies it is a useful promotional tool for others.

Annual general meetings

The Annual General Meeting (AGM) is a legal requirement for limited companies who have shareholders. It can be a brief meeting where annual financial results are presented to the shareholders and either accepted or rejected. It is also an opportunity for the shareholders to elect members of the board and to raise any other issues they think are important. The meeting can be a brief one where the board merely goes through the formalities or it can be a more positive occasion where the consultancy makes a presentation and reviews its activities.

Professional financial services

A professional adviser can carry out functions and provide a level of expertise that is not available within the consultancy. Accountants provide a basic bookkeeping service and can produce accounts for tax and for reporting; but increasingly they are diversifying their activities into business consultancy services. There is little distinction now between management consultancies and the larger firms of accountants. Management consultancies are traditionally involved in the areas of organization and business planning, but a new area of specialization is high technology. Their role is to evaluate your requirements, recommend solutions and, where necessary, implement their recommendations. Among the areas they cover are management organization, long-term planning for the consultancy, and high technology solutions to business problems. Banks too are diversifying their services away from the traditional role of lender and cashier; they supply a wide range of business and advisory services including payroll management and factoring.

Financial institutions

Financial institutions are a source of funds when you are borrowing money. They can also provide essential administrative services when you are raising capital by issuing shares or going public. Stockbrokers, for example, carry out all the necessary legal requirements and act on your behalf in preparing documents and issuing advertisements for the shares.

Solicitors

Solicitors are experts in legal matters, but they can also help you in a number of areas of financial management – determining conditions of employment, terms of business with suppliers or clients, specific contracts with clients, or agreements with landlords. They can also provide advice and action if you are involved in any dispute – chasing debtors, or in disagreements with clients or suppliers.

The Law Society is the professional body for solicitors; they can advise you on services available from their members.

Professional institutes

The two main professional institutes for the designer – the Chartered Society of Designers and the Design Business Group (DBG) – provide financial advisory services to members. DBG is planning to research professional fees and will help members with insurance and legal action in disputes. The Society has traditionally acted on its members' behalf in disputes. The professional bodies of accountants, solicitors, management consultants and financial institutes can help you to select the most suitable adviser and help you get the best from the professional service.

Crisis management

Financial mangement is concerned with providing the funds and cash to ensure that the company is financially sound. However, unforeseen problems can hit any company and, through no fault of its own, it gets into serious problems where it cannot meet its current obligations. Is the only course to go out of business? There are a number of courses of action that can be taken to avoid disaster. Problems like this tend to be of a short-term nature, for example, where projects have been cancelled or a client is unable to settle a large invoice. If the problem is longer term – shortage of cash or shortage of work – then the action you need to take should be more fundamental and will probably go beyond financial matters.

In the first place you should tell everyone involved what is going on; tell your debtors – the people who owe *you* money – that you need prompt settlement; tighten your credit control procedures. Try to secure payment by factoring, if that is possible, using the invoices as a guarantee. The second step is to tell your creditors – the people *you* owe money *to* – that you would like to postpone immediate payment in full to deal with the crisis. Take full advantage of normal terms of credit and explain why there is a temporary need to delay full settlement. The third stage is to involve your bankers, explaining the shortfall and supporting your argument with long-term trends and forecasts; the bank may be able to support you with a short-term loan or overdraft facility that meets your immediate requirements.

You then need to see how you can cope with recovering any particular debt. If a client refuses to pay a large bill, you may need to take legal action to recover it. As a last resort you can start looking at your own assets and resources and seeing how you can turn these into cash – selling property that you own, for example, cutting expansion or investment programmes, and finally making people redundant. The last solutions, however, affect the long-term development of your business; they can affect client confidence in your business and they can damage the morale of your own staff. Only use them as a last resort.

Financial health check

Finance is often discussed in terms of health. The following financial health-care check is designed to focus on those areas of your business finance where improvements could be made.

- *Income and expenditure* – do these balance, are you at least covering your costs?
- *Maximizing income* – are you getting the correct level of fees for the work you are doing, or are there alternative forms of payment that could be more profitable?

- *Cash flow* – are you invoicing quickly enough and exercising credit control to ensure fast receipt?
- *Funding* – have you got the right level of funding and are you getting the most efficient form of borrowing in terms of interest and tax performance?
- *Management information* – is the consultancy management fully aware of all aspects of business performance, and how up to date is the information?
- *Future requirements* – is the consultancy fully aware of its financial requirements in relation to its long-term plans?

FOUR
Personnel Management

One of the clichés about design and allied professions is that it is a people business. People are our greatest asset. A cliché it may be, but it is also true. A design group has few physical assets; it does not need machinery, although high technology equipment may change that; and it requires only a small amount of support equipment. Without the right people, however, the group could not function. The problem for the designer running a business is finding the right people, providing an environment in which they can work, and planning for future personnel needs.

Design education

An important base to design is a continuing group of new designers. In the majority of cases, they will come through the college system, so it is important to maintain close links between education and the professions. Some of these links are informal – where designers visit colleges to see student shows – but there are a number of colleges where designers are more closely involved, either as occasional lecturers or as professional advisers. Yet, many designers are quick to condemn colleges for providing students who are ill-equipped for the real world. So should there be closer links between education and the professionals, and what form would this take?

This book is not the place for a full discussion of design education, but there are two main types of course – degree and diploma. Although they vary in content they also vary in the emphasis they put on practical experience – the largest barrier between college and work. The courses can last from three to five years and combine general design training with specialist subjects like graphics, illustration or photography. At the end of the course the graduates should be able to take on a full range of studio work which is gradually tempered with practical experience. Holiday work in a studio is valuable experience for a student designer and this is one way in which design groups can make a contribution to education.

Recruiting graduates

Recruiting a graduate designer can be a risk for a small design consultancy, where every one must be productive from day one. In many ways, it is a

Catch 22 situation; commercial studios need people with experience but the pool of experienced people can only be renewed by giving newcomers a chance to prove themselves. There is a well established two way traffic between graduates and the professions. Students send their CVs and portfolios to studios and ask for an opportunity to present. Designers visit the degree shows to judge the work of a number of students and perhaps to make a preliminary assessment. What a professional is looking for in a student's portfolio is the ability to solve problems and to present the solutions in a clear and concise way. It is important to see concepts as well as printed specimens. This shows that the student's ideas are practical and that he can sustain an idea through to completion. In many cases the examples will be hypothetical – based on fictitious marketing situations – but it is important to know how the job relates to the brief. An exercise in pure style design is not design for the real world.

Recruiting students is a multi-stage process – the initial view of the portfolio, an interview, possibly a practical test and a trial period. This initial settling-in period is perhaps the most difficult time and and one where there is room for greater cooperation between consultancies and colleges. Many consultancies are represented on college advisory boards where they offer professional criticism of students' work and can give advice on work-related subjects. Other practices encourage members of their staff to go back to college to talk about their work experience. It is this transfer of experience that can be so valuable in bridging the gap between college and work.

Recruiting experienced staff

The problems of recruiting experienced staff are not so very different. You have a much greater choice of people, but the problem is to make the right decision. To start with you have to know who you are looking for. Just to recruit a designer is not sufficient. The designer must have a specific role to play and that will determine the job specification and the type of person you are looking for. In the job specification should be the type of work the designer will handle, what qualifications he should have and what kind of experience would be ideal. This gives you the basis of a recruitment advertisement and also helps you screen candidates when they first apply. There are a number of ways of recruiting experienced people – advertising the position, using a recruitment agency, or through informal contact. Advertising is the likely starting point and the most suitable media are *Campaign*, *Direction*, *Creative Review*, *Design Week* and *Graphics World*. *Design Week* and *Campaign* are the most flexible of these because they are weeklies. You can get an advertisement in quickly when a vacancy occurs and run a further insertion if the first candidates are not suitable. The others are monthly and you may have to wait a long time before the advertisement appears. The *Guardian* on Monday has a recruitment section called Creative and Media which covers publishing, theatre and the media as well as advertising, public relations and design. If you are looking for someone from your own locality advertising in the local press could be more appropriate.

The advertisement should state clearly what the position is, and the essential qualifications and experience. Some background information on the consultancy gives the candidates a flavour of what you are offering and helps to attract the right sort of candidate. Whether you quote a salary or other conditions is a matter of choice although senior positions are likely to be subject to negotiation. You should state clearly whether you want applicants to telephone or write in. For a relatively junior position you might ask candidates to send for an application form so that you can compare like with like. With senior staff you are looking for initiative and flair and you are likely to look for an individual contribution. The applications give you the first opportunity to screen candidates. Matching your job specification to the preliminary information should eliminate the unsuitable candidates.

The next stage is to interview suitable prospects to look at their portfolio and to discuss their working methods. Earlier in this section we discussed what to look for in a student's portfolio; the same comments apply here – you are looking for creative skills and the ability to take a concept through to completion. Does the portfolio indicate that the designer can handle the sort of work you specialize in? If, for example, you specialize in technical and industrial accounts, a designer whose background was in consumer packaging could have problems in making the transition. From the initial applications you will probably end up with a final shortlist of suitable candidates where you may find it hard to make a decision. What you have then to look for is the long-term potential of the candidates; how have they developed and which direction could they go in? What sort of contribution are they likely to make to the practice? The right candidate is the one with the greatest potential (see Chapter 6, page 97).

Using a recruitment consultancy, you can cut out some of the preliminary stages and save yourself a lot of time. The consultancy either runs its own advertisements specific to the job or refers to people already on its books. These are people who have indicated an interest in moving jobs and keep in touch with the job market through the consultancy. Their role is to give you a shortlist of suitable people of the right calibre. You then go through the selection process, and if you take on one of their candidates you pay the consultancy a fee for the introduction. This could be a one-off fee or it might be based on a percentage of the first year salary.

A third category of recruitment consultant is the executive search consultant or head hunter. They are looking for top people for senior positions. They contact the person you are looking for and tell him about the position – preparing the way for more a formal interview. Their services are normally charged on a fee basis but they can be worthwhile for getting the right person.

Staff training

Recruiting the right person is the first stage in building a staff that meets your present and future objectives. Marketing conditions are never static so you need to be adaptable to change. Further training could be an important asset, and one of the growth areas is likely to be training in new technology.

Computer graphics, electronic page make-up systems, electronic retouching, paintboxes and typesetting direct to disc are already part of the high technology studio, but few people are qualified to operate them, so a studio may not be getting the full benefit of its investment.

A number of colleges now include computer graphics in their degree and diploma courses, while others offer postgraduate courses for the professions. A number of private organizations provide general or tailor-made courses which are held in local venues or in your own studio. Equipment manufacturers provide initial demonstrations and also organize seminars to show how their equipment can be used. They provide training services for people operating the equipment, although the training may be practical rather than creative. The emphasis in college courses is on the creative uses of the equipment rather than the data processing aspects. Although designers are less likely to be directly involved, it is important to keep up to date with developments in related industries. Typesetting, origination and printing technology all have an effect on the finished results a designer can achieve (see Chapter 5, page 82).

Working environment

Getting and training the right people is part of the personnel management process, but equally important is providing the right conditions for working. This would include an environment that is conducive to good work, stimulating work, a flexible organization that allows people to progress and develop and reasonable working conditions, a difficult balancing act when the pressure is on to produce good design against a continuous series of deadlines. The working environment is an intangible covering factors like location, furnishing, office layouts and general working conditions. A studio is a working environment; it should be practical area but it does not need to be too industrial. Many studios see their office as part of their overall corporate identity and employ architects or interior designers to create the right working environment. A consultancy like Pentagram that includes architecture in its activities accepts that as natural, and their premises should serve as an example of simple and functional, but elegant, accommodation. The environment helps to set the tone for the whole studio – it should be a reflection of the work that the consultancy does, and both clients and staff should be aware of it.

A good environment makes an important contribution to staff morale. So too does the type and level of work going through the studio. One studio took a conscious decision to handle only work that they felt happy with. They dropped some existing clients and turned down any work that they could not do on their own terms. Some might call it commercial suicide but the studio prospered and the staff were delighted with their working arrangements. Pentagram called their book *Living by Design* and explained the philosophy behind their work. What was important was the sense of leadership the partners gave. Each was a leader in his field and continued to demonstrate their ability. They were working partners and they led by example.

Working relationships

But what of the staff who handle the rest of the day-to-day work, how do they relate to senior staff and how can they be motivated to produce their best work? Though it is important to establish clear lines of organization, this process – like management – should be invisible. In a small consultancy, where there are partners and staff, the relationships are simple: there are straight lines of communications. But, in a larger group, where there are large numbers of staff designers, you have to make decisions about their relationship. Who are the senior designers – is it age or experience that counts? What sort of mix do you have within a group? Is it a mix of age and experience or do you mix people of different abilities and functions? Much depends on the type of work you handle. A mix of skills and abilities makes you more flexible and able to cope with a variety of tasks. But if you handle a large volume of work that is similar, you need a group of people who can cope with the workload.

Delegation and progress control is an important consideration when you have large numbers of people working on projects. They will not all be constantly busy, so you need careful planning to get the best possible work flow. Jobs progress through design, approval, artwork and final approval stages. This means they are not constantly occupied and can fit in other projects in between. What you need to look for is that the workload is spread evenly. Some people will work faster than others so there may be an unfair allocation of work. Chapter 5 on project management discusses work flow patterns.

Where the workload is heavy, you may need a production manager to keep work in progress moving smoothly. The relationship between designers and progress people is not always a smooth one and it needs a careful organization structure to preserve the right working atmosphere. Within a large group of designers there are a number of possible relationships. You can have designers who handle complete projects from design through to completion and take full responsibility for all production work. Alternatively you can employ people who are purely conceptual designers and who hand their work over to other people for the later stages. You could group senior and junior designers together in small loose groups so that projects are split and the junior people benefit from the experience of working with senior designers. The relationship may be more formal as groups of designers work with senior partners on particular groups of accounts or on special activities. Pentagram, for example, has a structure where a group of designers work with a partner concentrating on the separate disciplines of architecture, product design and graphic design. The different groups share central resources but are otherwise autonomous.

Support staff

When you are building up a design group it is not just designers you need. Design, like any other business, needs support staff to function efficiently. The question is whether to employ the support staff on a full-time basis or part-time. Support staff are not earning income in the sense that designers are, but they are essential to the organization. Accounting staff, for example, who keep the books used to be essential to even the smallest organization, but with the introduction of computerized accounting systems their routine bookkeeping function has become less important. Financial planning is no less important and, if the partners do not have this capability, you could use an accountant on a part-time basis. His services would be limited to checking the accounts, preparing cash flow forecasts and financial statements and giving financial advice when necessary. The accountant can also carry out the role of a company secretary.

Consultants

Consultancies can advise you on those areas of the business that you are unfamiliar with. Michael Peters called in Bob Silver to set up financial management systems when his group was suffering financial losses. Looked at in a broad sense, there are many areas where professional advice can prove valuable – finance, marketing, corporate planning, interior design and personnel management. A consultant is a complement to your own resources, someone who allows you to get on with what you are best at – providing a design service. The crossover point between using consultants and employing staff specialists comes when you find out you need to consult the experts regularly. At that point, their services have become an essential part of your business.

Terms and conditions of employment

Whether you run a small or large design group you have legal obligations to your employees. Personnel management is an important function that all employees have to comply with. Every employee should have his own terms and conditions of employment defined. This covers broad areas like working hours, holiday arrangements, notice to be given and other conditions. In a business like design where you are dealing with confidential information you should build in terms about confidentiality. Overtime can be a tricky subject and you should lay down clear guidelines about this. Employees have rights over dismissal; you have to give certain periods of notice and these are related to length of service. If you find yourself in a situation where you have to make someone redundant, there are statutory periods of notice you have to adhere to. A full guide to the rules and regulations is given in books on personnel management.

Personnel management and new technology

A good designer looks at every aspect of a client's problem. The designer has to work hard to get full value. It's the same with the design business. The consultancy should look at every aspect of its business to see how it can improve – either improving its own efficiency or the service it is able to offer clients. It is surprising how a small change in routine activities can affect your efficiency – transferring telephone calls automatically, computerizing progress and accounting, changing the working layout – all simple enough in themselves. By looking critically at each aspect of the business it is possible to pinpoint the prime areas for improvement. Of all the factors that can affect business efficiency the introduction of the computer has had the most profound effect. Automating administration, taking over routine mechanical functions in the studio, or adding new levels of sophistication to studio facilities, it could take the studio into a new era.

Computers in design

A computer by itself is simply a unit for processing data; it has no functions without data or instructions. In the 1980s more and more software packages are available which are ready for immediate use – packages for word processing, computer graphics, accounting. There is no lack of software but you have to choose packages that are compatible with your processing equipment. Software houses not unnaturally design their packages for systems that are widely used. A system that has little software written for it could become an inflexible and expensive liability. You should also make sure that the system has the capacity to cope with increasing workload, or that it can be upgraded. Although manufacturers do not deliberately build in obsolescence, the pace of technological change is very rapid and you could find your system trailing behind that of competitors. As an alternative to ready-made software packages you can use a software consultancy to develop programs specially for your application. You specify the function, and they design a program to handle it.

Studio accounting

In the section on recording and charging, a tailor-made system for monitoring studio costs was discussed. This is the electronic equivalent of a job bag and gives studios up-to-date information on time and costs spent on a job. There are other standard business accounting packages that can be used for invoicing, bookkeeping and payroll functions, though they do not have the inbuilt monitoring capability that the studio system has. An accounting system should give you access to financial information about your practice, giving you an up-to-date picture of profitability and cash flow. It should be an aid to financial management as well as a simple bookkeeping service (see Chapter 3, page 53).

Project management

Another package can help you to control the progress of work through the studio. A project control system allows you to set up a network for complex projects, showing the order in which parts of the job have to be completed, and giving lead times for each. By monitoring actual progress against planned target dates you can keep a check on the job to see whether there are any bottlenecks and whether the job can be completed on time. Project control would not be needed on every job, but it is ideal for long-term, complex, corporate identity, retail or exhibition programmes where the timescale is large, and many different elements contribute to the job (see Chapter 5, page 86).

Text processing

Text processing is now a standard feature of most computing systems, and can make a contribution to cost saving and productivity. In the early stages of text preparation you can carry out extensive amendments without retyping the whole text – ideal when you are working on a lengthy document. When the final text is approved you can use the disc to go direct to typesetting. There is a standard code, called ASPIC, which is used to give instructions to the typesetter. It covers paragraphing, levels of heading, and many other typographic functions. Your typesetter can give you details.

Typesetting direct from disc can be economical for long documents, because you avoid double keying where the typesetter rekeys a text that has already been typed. The typeset text should also be accurate and should not need proofreading if the original was correct. Author's corrections, however, can quickly reduce these economies because the typesetter has to spend time searching out the changes and dealing with them manually.

Design systems

Where the computer is likely to make the most direct contribution is in its handling of repetitive design work and advanced experimental work. In the 1970s Pentagram designed the Barbour Index using a computer program linked to traditional design skills. By establishing a standard page grid and storing the formula and text on computer they were able to produce an integrated consistent looking publication which could be easily updated despite the vast amount of information. Whole page make-up is slowly gaining acceptance in the newspaper industry. Here text, headlines, half tones and lines elements are all set in position on the screen so that the editor or designer can preview the layout and make any necessary adjustments. More sophisticated equipment has the facilities to show tints, reversals, cut outs, vignettes and other creative effects.

Scaled-down versions of the page layout system can be used to tackle smaller page sizes like standard A4. They can be linked to typesetting systems so that typesetting output can be used as direct input to the page make-up system. At the other end an electronic scanner can take page output and transparencies, scanning and separating the camera-ready artwork into digital form for origination. The same equipment can be used to work on transparencies or other colour subjects, electronic retouching, changing colours, image enhancement, and scaling – work which would normally be put out to a photographic specialist. At the top end of the scale are computer graphics installations like the paintbox. Corporate and financial institutions use them for their graphics capabilities, rapidly converting statistical data into graphics. They can also be used for producing computer-generated images, animated logos and some extra-ordinary creative effects. With a price tag of around £100,000 this is unlikely to become universal studio equipment.

The computer has been widely described as the key to the paperless office; in a studio it seems unlikely to take such as advanced role. But designers can expect an increased level of electronic support for their creative activities. Certainly at the mechanical stage, the traditional process of paste-up and conventional pre-press would seem to be limited. A typical work cycle would be creative design and writing, text processing and setting from disc, in-line page make-up, transparency retouching and scanning, with proof printing on a laser printer.

Building in-house facilities

With so much emphasis on in-house facilities this suggests that the studio of the future could be a much more integrated business handling most of the work that was previously put out to specialist suppliers. There is a dividing line between in-house and bought-in facilities which is normally an economic one, i.e. when the volume of work is high install your own facilities. There should be enough throughput to cover the running costs of the equipment and perhaps make a contribution to the company's profitability. Volume is not the only consideration; sometimes the speed or quality of service from outside suppliers may not be sufficient. In that case handling the work yourself could be the solution. Products or services where you are looking for a uniform high quality and consistent standard are the ideal ones to bring in-house. So a PMT camera, phototypesetting equipment or a rostrum camera could be a good investment, but employing your own illustrator or photographer would not be because you are looking for variety in approach and style, and you are unlikely to get that from one person.

Bringing equipment and services in-house means a number of changes in organization. You may need to take on new staff with the skills to operate the equipment. This adds to overhead costs but it could also form the basis of a new profit centre where you sell the service to outsiders. So long as this does not affect the content and quality of your own supplies it can be a useful addition to income.

Electronic delivery

Business efficiency does not need to be concerned with major purchases or investment in computerization. Sometimes simple changes like the introduction of a facsimile machine could save a great deal of time and effort. A facsimile machine would allow you to transmit documents to clients with their own compatible equipment almost instantaneously. That can save postal delays and courier charges, and help you get rapid response on queries and approval on urgent jobs. Electronic mail facilities built onto an existing computer system can achieve the same results. Although the popular systems cannot yet handle the transmission of graphics, that development cannot be far away. For the rapid transmission of text, instructions or routine correspondence, however, there is no faster method.

Investing for expansion

Internal changes can affect the way you run your business. The important thing is to relate the improvements and the investment to your business expansion plans. Investment in one area could be wasted if you then expanded in another direction. Chapter 6 on expansion shows how to build up integrated plans, while chapter 3 on financial management discusses ways to evaluate the cost-benefit of an investment.

FIVE
Project Management

Project management has now become one of the critical activities in design; a consultancy is judged as much on its ability to complete a project on time and within budget as it is on the quality of its design solutions. When the International Design Group came to the UK, its success in winning the Gateshead Metro project – a massive retail complex – owed much to its native North American experience in managing similar projects. Retail in particular is the design discipline where good project management skills are essential. When Conran Design refurbished British Home Stores, the conversion of a national chain of branches had to be completed over a single weekend; and that after a very rapid design development. Conran had a background in retail projects and it had considerable resources to draw on.

Project management skills should not be confined to the larger consultancies. It came as an initial surprise to the design establishment when Peter Leonard Associates won a contract to redesign a small number of WH Smith flagship branches, but it was a real surprise when they were awarded a contract to complete the national programme. The consultancy did not dramatically increase in size to handle the project; much depended on project management efficiency. Clients in the retail sector demand this level of efficiency; in the past they have enjoyed this service from architects, and there is a growing service in independent professional project management available from quantity surveyors. In a report on future prospects in retail centre development, the large financial institutions who fund retail centres praised the design industry's creative skills, but expressed concern at the apparent lack of professionalism and resources to handle major projects (see Chapter 1, page 9).

The client demands professionalism, but efficient project management benefits the consultancy as well. It ensures that you only commit the right level of resources to the workload. The spate of redundancies in large consultancies in 1986 showed how important it is to get the numbers right. Using the right number of staff efficiently helps to build profit. Good project management helps you complete work quickly and efficiently, leaving you free to take on more work and increase turnover. Most important of all, efficient project management puts you in contention for the large complex projects. Project management need not just apply to large projects or to retail; it can be applied at any level. As soon as a designer gets beyond the design stage he is a project manager. On a simple brochure, for example, the designer has to coordinate the activities of writers, photographers, illustrators, typesetters, finished artists and printer.

With the continued success of design, the trend to larger projects should continue. In the late 1980s corporate identity has once again become a major design activity. The corporate identity programmes of the 1960s and 1970s are due for revision and their implementation provides a major project management challenge. In the financial sector, banks and building societies are carrying out major refurbishments to build their competitive edge. At the time of writing most of the projects were at pilot stage, but the plans were to go national, so the volume and the pace of work is likely to increase. Retail was the major growth area and here the cycle of changes seemed to grow ever shorter. High street redesign predominated in the 1980s, but shopping centre refurbishment and out-of-town retail operations are still high on the list of design buyers (see Chapter 2, page 22). In these conditions, the practice has to be efficient to survive.

The importance of project management has also led to a more complex relationship with suppliers. The designer's role is no longer confined to the drawing board. Exhibition designers, for example, stress that theirs is a specialist activity. Graphic design skills are not enough; their responsibility extends to the exhibition site – negotiating with organizers and supervising the work of contractors.

The consultancy AID's product development programmes begin with market research, design, consumer testing, type approval and production engineering. Projects have to be carefully planned to fit in with the client's own manufacturing programmes. AID has solved part of the coordination problem by setting up an internal research department to cut out a complex supplier relationship. Project management has an important role to play in making full use of these resources.

A designer is an organizer; he does not carry out all the work on a project, but coordinates the activities of a number of different specialists. To handle a project efficiently, you have to know your supplier's abilities and limitations and know how to get the best out of them. Project management is the process of organizing time, people and resources to complete a budget on time and within budget. Many different skills are needed:

- Planning
- Analytical – to establish a good brief
- Organizational – to manage people and time
- Financial understanding – to control costs
- Coordinating – to select and monitor suppliers.

To illustrate the different stages a project can progress through, we have used the example of brochure in the following sections. In different design disciplines, a project would progress through the same basic stages.

The importance of client briefing

Good design depends as much on good clients as on good designers. From your client you need a good brief, an attitude that is sympathetic to good design, and firm control to steer a project through a number of internal approval stages. Good client relations start at the initial briefing. Get the wrong brief, and any work you do will be off target. A brief should be comprehensive; it should be realistic about what the project can achieve. The client's brief should explain why the product is used, the product's position and the marketing plan. It should give the designer a clear framework in which to operate. You need to make sure that you are given sufficient information to handle the project properly. It helps to know what information you are looking for so that you can steer the briefing in the right direction. It is not sufficient to be asked to produce an A4 brochure that includes a selection of photographs and a piece of text. That is a layout, not an exercise in design. The copy and the photographs, if they are established, should come at a later date. What you need to establish at the outset is the reason for the brochure – its objective.

Objectives

A good company policy is to ask anyone who wants a brochure to establish a business case for it – before the initial briefing. The business case describes the market the campaign is aimed at, the product that is being launched, the importance of the market and the anticipated profit. It should also cover the way the product is to be marketed and how the proposed brochure or other form of promotion fits into the marketing programme. Is it to be delivered by the sales force or mailed out alone? Is it to be given away on an exhibition stand or will it form part of a composite mailing or presentation with other publications? All of this information helps to give the brochure a communications task and defines the level of detail that it has to carry.

Content

Only then should you move to the question of content. You need information on the people who are going to buy the product – what role does it have in their business and what benefits is it likely to give them? Benefits are not the same as product features; customers who buy a machine for their factory are buying a means of manufacturing their own product more efficiently – a way of improving factory productivity. They are not buying new integrated circuit control or a polished aluminium finish. The features are the means by which the machine can improve productivity, but they may be of little interest to the person who is reading the brochure.

For that reason you need to establish the reader's level of knowledge and his part in the decision-making process. If you are designing publications for industrial products, you will be aiming at different levels of buyer. Take a sophisticated product like a computer. The decision to buy is taken at a number of different levels, and the message must be precisely tailored for each. The executive manager decides on the broad requirements of the system; he is not really interested in functional performance. The departmental manager wants to know how the system operates, what level of performance it gives him, how easy it is to use and how it will benefit the department. At the user level, the reader is concerned with the operation of the system – what the functions are in detail and how they are used. The user version of the brochure is operating at a high level of detail.

Identity

Other practical considerations should be covered in the briefing. One is the question of identity – how the new publication relates to others from the same company. There may be an established corporate identity to follow or other publications to be used in the same marketing exercise. New publications have to be in sympathy.

Budgets and timing

You also need to set broad budgets before carrying out design work. What quantities of the publication are needed and what budget is available for the project? Although it is difficult to get a basis for costing at this early stage, a broad budget figure can eliminate some of the design options. With the budget forecast goes a project timetable – an indication of the final delivery date, together with intermediate dates when material or information will be available (see Chapter 3, page 47).

Briefing documents

After the briefing meeting it is useful to summarize the main responsibilities and activities in a briefing document. This lets everyone involved in the project know what has been discussed and what is planned. Professional clients insist that this briefing document is approved before any more work is carried out on the project, eliminating the risk of unwarranted criticism at a later stage in the project.

Getting a brief from the right person

Despite all the effort you make to get the information you need, you may find that you have been briefed by the wrong person, or that someone else will be your contact during the project. Initial meetings, including the briefing, are likely to be with publicity professionals, but they may be acting on someone else's behalf. The sales manager, technical manager or some other client within the company needs a publication, and uses the professionals as a service department to get professional advice and access to the right suppliers. It is also important from the company's point of view to have all publication work coordinated so that corporate identity and budgetary control are maintained (see Chapter 2, page 32). By dealing with a publicity professional, you should get a sound brief initially, but there are dangers at a later approval stage that the person initiating the project may not agree with your interpretation of the brief, or indeed with the publicity professional's interpretation of it. That is why a briefing document is so important. If you experience the problem of approvals on one project, it is in your interests to ask for a different form of briefing and to insist that everyone involved in the project is present at the meeting.

If you are dealing with the client directly and handle the project yourself, you are in control, but, as organizations grow, the problem of delegation and communication arise. Design groups tackle this problem in different ways. Some believe that only the principals or senior designers should be involved in client contact, and that they should coordinate the project internally, briefing other designers and monitoring progress. This may work well from an administrative point of view, but it reduces the time the principals can spend on design work. In an article in *Creative Review*, principals from a number of design consultancies gave their views on this problem. Those that were trying to handle both administration and design work found that they were working an exceptionally long day; they felt frustrated because they had little time to design themselves. If the consultancy has developed a design style that is led by the principals the administrative burden can be a problem.

An alternative is to appoint an account handler or project manager who is not directly involved in design, but understands the design process – not an easy combination to find. Nor is it a practical proposition unless there is a regular flow of work. An account handler – in the strict sense – is an unproductive person, his time is not chargeable, although a figure to cover this should be built into the cost of the job. If you are only handling a small number of projects, then much of an account handler's time will be unused. Another drawback is that there is no direct contact between client and designer – a situation that is not ideal. However, a studio with a high ratio of routine design and artwork to creative design, and a large number of clients need someone to deal with clients – someone who can feed the work through and let the studio get on with turning the work round quickly.

Another possibility is to allow individual designers to deal directly with clients. This has a number of advantages: the designer is able to explain his work to the client and to defend it against unfair criticism – a process which can often be difficult for a third person. It does take experience though to be able to present your work convincingly and not all designers welcome the challenge. It also takes nerve to stand up to difficult clients and there are occasions when the criticism could be destructive. The client is in a difficult situation when he has to criticize directly the person who created the work. The mutual embarrassment could create an artificial environment where the client gets a job that he doesn't really want and the long-term future of the account is put at risk. The other disadvantage is that it takes the designer away from the drawing board; when the workload is heavy this could lead to a reduction in efficiency and profitability.

The way you handle the business depends on a number of factors – the personality of the people in your organization, their workload, the type of work you handle and the professionalism of your clients.

Briefing – the client's responsibility

A good brief is essentially a partnership between designer and client. The client has responsibility for providing information and support at various stages of the project. As the section on project management practice shows, design management is becoming increasingly more professional. The essential requirements for a good client are:

- An understanding of the designer's information needs
- The authority to get approvals at the right level
- An understanding of the design process
- An understanding of design's relation to other disciplines.

The client should have the authority to make decisions that will keep the project moving and should know when and when not to get involved in the design process.

Progressing a project

Projects progress through many different stages after the initial briefing. To simplify the presentation the project taken as an example here is a brochure. Other types of project would follow a similar route.

Creative proposals

After the initial briefing the project can take a number of different directions. You may be presented with a complete kit of parts – text, photographs, and an agreed brief. The project is simple in design terms; if you feel that solution is right for the client, you can go straight to detailed layout. But, a far more satisfactory brief is to prepare creative proposals with no specific input from the client. This is a true design exercise; the client gives you a communications problem and your task is to select the right combination of words and pictures to solve the problem.

Before you get too far with detailed layout, you have to get approval for your creative proposals. These are like the architect's impressions of a building. They are not detailed plans but an indication of the direction of the design – the way it tackles the problem. They can take the form of rough visuals, a written proposal, or a combination of both. The choice depends on the complexity of the project. A literature system, for example, is a way of organizing information so that a message communicates at every target level. In the early stages, layout is less important than organization. What part does each element play in the system? How does it meet its objectives? What should the contents of each publication be? Only when you have solved those problems should you move onto detailed design considerations. Overall visual identity would be the second stage in the creative proposals; elements such as photography or illustration form the other part. The creative proposals should form an outline or structure to which you can add the detail of layout, copy, photographs and illustration.

The creative proposal stage is useful for estimating. When the client asks you for a budget you usually have little idea of the form the brochure will take – how many photographs, pages or how much text. Any budget figures you give are purely guesses. When you have had creative proposals accepted, you get a firm basis for estimating because you have a plan to work to. It has the added advantage that you don't spend too much time on work that might be wasted. If the creative proposals have to be changed, that is the only cost incurred. Whether you can charge for the additional creative work depends on your relationship with the client (see Chapter 3, page 48).

Approvals

When you submit creative proposals, you first come across the problem of approvals. You may find out that more than one person has to approve the work. Unfortunately, these people do not always give their comments in the early stages or they may change their minds later. Many clients find it difficult to give an opinion until they see a publication in familiar form – as camera-ready artwork, for example, or, worse still, at page proof stage. Publicity professionals who deal with designers regularly can offer comment at any stage but, where a managing director or finance director gets involved, their inexperience can cause problems.

The number of approvers increases in proportion to the sensitivity of a project. The annual report to shareholders is perhaps the most fearsome. As well as design and copy approvals from a publicity professional, you need technical approval from the people responsible for finance; senior management approval on policy statements; and public relations and board approval to give the corporate viewpoint. Unfortunately, you don't have to get agreement at just one stage – but each time an amendment is made. On an annual report this can be frequent.

To reduce the problems to manageable proportions you should agree a system for approvals with your client. You need to list everyone who should comment, the stage at which they should be involved and the limit of their authority. On a product brochure, for example, it would be sensible to complete all technical approvals before getting legal and corporate approvals. Qestions of design should be confined to publicity professionals because you could end up with seven or eight entirely different comments on your design – a difficult problem to reconcile. You also need to formalize the way you get approvals. Your main contact in the company should coordinate all the comments from within the company, giving you one marked version with the correct signatures on it. Whether you use stick-on labels or get the client to sign the visual, galleys, artwork, or proofs doesn't really matter. What is important is that you get the right clearance at each stage.

Later stages

From the acceptance of the creative proposals you are working on a strategy that has been agreed with your client. The brochure can now take a number of different directions. You have to prepare detail design proposals, draft text, and plan any elements of photography or illustration. These stages can progress in parallel or they could be integrated. It depends on the working method you prefer.

Balancing the workload

It is unlikely that your workload would consist of only one brochure, so you need to be careful how you schedule work. A brochure goes through detail design, copy, type mark-up, proofreading, camera-ready artwork, print specification and colour proof stages. But the designer's true involvement varies with each stage; there would be relatively long stages of concentrated effort at detail design and camera-ready artwork stage, but between those stages there would be periods of client approval when there would be no studio involvement.

Production stages

Planning becomes increasingly important as projects become more complex and the workload increases. It ensures that your forecasts to clients are feasible and accurate, and that you are fully utilizing your resources. Copy and design can coveniently be submitted for approval at the same stage. If they are both approved you can move safely on to the production stage where you start to involve outside suppliers. Here a project becomes more complicated because progress is outside your control. Work inside the studio can be scheduled to meet client commitments as you see them, but when you are dealing with suppliers they also have priorities and schedules and may not regard your work as their most urgent task. However, the more money you spend with a supplier the more influence you have over delivery dates and priority treatment, so discuss delivery with your supplier before you prepare schedules.

Dealing with suppliers

Dealing with suppliers also creates extra administration. On a brochure you have to brief suppliers, approve their work, check progress, issue orders, deal with invoices and make sure their work is integrated with your own. This is the designer as organizer – coordinating the activities of other people. The list of suppliers involved on a brochure could be extensive – writers, illustrations, photographers, retouchers, typesetters, process houses and printers. As a designer, you depend on good relationships with your suppliers. To get the best from their services you should be aware that you have a choice of suppliers and that their working methods and techniques vary considerably. Since technology plays an increasingly important part in all aspects of the design business, it is important to keep up to date with developments among your suppliers.

Typesetters

Typesetting is an area where the greatest penetration of new technology has taken place. You judge a typesetter as much on his equipment as on his reputation and service. Phototypesetting in its various forms has become the industry standard. Inevitably there are enough variations in the industry to make the term standard redundant; each process has its own characteristics in terms of quality, speed of output, cost suitability and compatability with the other elements in graphic reproduction. From the typesetter's point of view flexibility, productivity and economy are more important considerations, but for a designer it has to be quality of setting, choice of fonts and facilities such as kerning, variable character width and line spacing – all at a reasonable rate. More and more fonts are available for phototypesetting equipment so there is no lack of choice. Typesetting equipment manufacturers publish guides to their typeface ranges and issue frequent bulletins giving up-to-date information on faces that have recently been added. Some machines have the added capability of digitizing graphic images such as logotypes and even half tone material, as well as a full range of rules and borders.

There is a growth in the number of typesetters accepting client's word-processing discs as direct input to the typesetting system. Here the client keys in his own text and adds instructions to the disc; this is known as formatting the disc and there is now an industry standard code known as the ASPIC code. The process of typesetting from word processing discs is known as single keystroking and it aims to increase economy and efficiency by eliminating two stages of typesetting – text entry and proofreading. Any errors are treated as author's correction so you need to maintain high standards of reading. Typesetters should not have to read direct entry text, although they should check the setting for typographical accuracy. Correcting a text that was innacurate on the original disc can destroy many of the cost advantages. Making corrections means time spent searching the disc for the faulty section and the cost of running out new prints of the setting.

Setting from disc provides cost advantage when accurate text of the right length goes through without any further amendment. At present texts of more than thirty-two pages A4 are economical. You can also add together smaller jobs such as four eight-page A4 folders – the important thing is that they are on the same disc. There is a minimum charge for reading a disc, regardless of the length of text. Smaller jobs below thirty-two pages are best suited to traditional typesetting methods. The type of discs you submit can also affect cost. Current systems are designed to accept a 3½ or 5¼ inch floppy disc; unfortunately not all word processors operate on those sizes (see also Chapter 4, page 72). To deal with this problem the typesetter uses a device known as a multidisc reader which can read discs that would otherwise be incompatible.

Choosing a typesetter involves balancing a number of different considerations – economy, quality of setting, speed of delivery and service. Many of these factors are determined by the typesetter's level of technological innovation. Buying the right machinery can make a tremendous difference, so it pays to keep up to date with developments that your suppliers are making. You can get information on typesetters from a directory such as *The Creative Handbook* or from editorial features in magazines like *Printing World* or *Lithoweek*. Most typesetters will supply typesheets and manuals giving information on the range of faces available and on their equipment capability.

Writers

Few design groups employ full-time writers; most rely on freelance writers or use copy supplied by the client. On many types of project, the writer's contribution may be an important one – not just editing copy to fit the layout or ensuring consistency but in helping to solve communications problems through the right balance of text and illustration. When you are working on publications or projects that involve considerable amounts of text, get the writer involved at an early stage. Writers like designers have different specialities. The good advertising copywriter can rarely adapt to publication work, where the skill is to organize information rather than condense a complicated story into a brief persuasive piece of copy that has to grab the attention and create an immediate response. The two skills are very different. A writer should be able to show examples of his finished work; the balance of his portfolio should indicate the medium he prefers.

Although there is no definitive way of assessing a writer's work you can learn a lot from the finished project – how well has the text integrated with the design, does it contribute to the effective communication of a message, is the message reinforced with good subheads and captions? The skills of a writer who specializes in audio-visual are very different. The writer needs to have technical as well as creative skills and the ability to work with other audio-visual suppliers. Few script writers are likely to have had the luxury of show reels to show finished programmes, so you have to rely on judging finished scripts and the writer's credentials.

Your involvement with a freelance writer can be at a number of levels. First the writer needs a brief. You need to decide whether you can supply all the information a writer needs or whether your client should brief the writer direct. As well as discussing the objectives of the project, the writer will need detailed factual information on the product, market and prospects. If it is a complex technical subject, the need for direct briefing will be even greater. After the briefing you can ask the writer to prepare text in isolation or to work closely with you on creative concepts. There are many advantages in having writers and designers working together on a project, although it is not always practical when you are using a freelance. Apart from practical considerations of copy fit and overall structure, writers can help to give shape to a designer's ideas. The process of creating a brochure, exhibition or audio-visual programme should perhaps be called information design, with both writer and designer contributing to the solution.

You also need to deal with practical matters such as schedules, costs and responsibilities for approvals. Writers, like designers, have different methods of charging for their work. Some will give a fixed price for the job while other will quote an hourly rate, and give you a cost summary at the end of the project. You should still ask for an estimate even on a long complex project but the accuracy of the estimate will depend on how the job has been defined. Freelance writers advertise their services in magazines like *Creative Review* and *Design and Art Direction*.

Photographers

The choice of photographer is almost as wide as the choice of designer. They specialize in fashion, portraiture, location work, editorial, industrial reportage, product and almost any other category you can think of. Their premises range from the massive drive-in studio to no studio at all, while the quality of their work will vary enormously and is to some extent dictated by the equipment they have available. Rates vary in a scale running from the top London studios to a local photographer handling mainly industrial work. You have to define the photographs you need and choose the right photographer for the job – not an easy task when all you have to go on is a portfolio of previous work. The balance of the portfolio will indicate the type of work that the photographer is capable of. Great still life photographers are often unhappy working with models on location because so many factors are outside their control.

You can make an initial shortlist of suitable photographers from the numerous photography directories that are available. They include directories showing the spread of work by a number of different photographers, and yearbooks showing award winning work during that year or work which the directory thinks is commendable. Photographers' agents are another source of information. They represent the interest of a group of different photographers and visit design groups and agencies regularly to try to build up work for their clients. Agents take a percentage of the photographer's fees for securing the work.

Different photographers have their own methods of charging for their work. Most will charge for the time spent on the job at an hourly, half day or daily rate. Travel and accommodation costs would be charged extra. If they hire special equipment or lighting or even a special studio for the project, they will charge for that and they will also bill you for materials and processing. Model fees and the services of a make-up artist would also be extra.

The photographer's brief should include the type of shots and feeling you are looking for, with a visual for reference if possible. The format of the shot (portrait or landscape or a selection of both), the process (transparency or print) and transparency size, together with a schedule – all this is important information. Some photographers prefer to work under close direction while others are happy to take a brief and return the shots to you when they are finished. You need to discuss the question of art direction and allow for it in your costings.

Location work can create different problems. You have to make arrangements with the people on site to make sure that equipment is available and ready for photography. You should establish a contact on site for the photographer and if necessary arrange security clearance. Travelling directions and details of address and telephone number are also essential. Photographers who take on extensive location work with a lot of travelling and high material costs may ask for payment in advance, or quick settlement of their invoices because of cash flow problems.

Record-keeping

Time is the designer's greatest asset; it is the commodity you have to sell, so it must be carefully monitored and recorded. You should aim to charge as much of your time as possible to a client, and be able to account for it. A comprehensive recording system is essential to make sure that all chargeable time is recorded and allocated to the correct client.

Chargeable costs

Before you set up a system, you need to know the scope of the charges to be included. What often surprises designers is the relatively small proportion of their time that they actually spend at the drawing board. Because the designer is an organizer – coordinating the services of many other suppliers – much of his time will be spent attending meetings, briefing people, approving their work and commenting on progress, writing orders, checking invoices and coordinating all the different elements. To see just where the time goes, we will consider below two projects that are typical of the work designers handle – a corporate brochure and an exhibition stand. In both cases, we assume that the designer has total responsibility for the project from initial concept through to completion. In these examples, no attempt is made to quantify the time spent at each stage – every project is different. But what emerges clearly is that there is more than just design time involved; to estimate projects such as these you have to be very careful in your forecast of the time spent on other activities. For example, travelling to meetings, writing reports, briefing suppliers, checking invoices, and monitoring costs against budgets seems to bear little relation to designing a brochure, but the activities represent time spent on a client's behalf – time that could be spent earning money on other projects. That time must be recorded and charged. Whether you charge service time at the same hourly rate as design time is a matter for discussion with the client, but jobs that are high on administration and low on design content could prove unprofitable if you set your service rate too low (see Chapter 3, page 46).

Time involvement in publication design

Publications in their various forms are likely to be a significant part of the designer's output. The corporate brochure represents a prestigious project for both client and designer, and for that reason, administrative time and quality control will be concentrated. A corporate brochure will also encompass most aspects of publication design and production – photography, copy, illustration, and full colour printing as well as design, artwork, and print management. The principles of time involvement can readily be transferred to other types of publication.

This is the likely sequence of events with all the hidden extras included:

Initial briefing
(1) Meeting.
(2) Write meeting note.
(3) Set up job file.

Creative and budget proposals
(1) Planning content.
(2) Prepare visuals.
(3) Forecast design, artwork and materials costs.
(4) Estimates from photographer, illustrator, typesetter, writer.
(5) Prepare print specification, get print estimate.
(6) Prepare budget.

Presentation of proposals
(1) Meeting.
(2) Write report and budget forecasts.
(3) Meeting report.

Detailed briefing/planning
(1) Meeting.
(2) Research library photographs.
(3) Prepare location shot list/arrange clearance through client.
(4) Prepare photographic schedule.
(5) Brief photographer/check availablity.
(6) Get references for photographer.
(7) Select and brief illustrator.
(8) Discuss copy content.
(9) Select and brief writer.
(10) Prepare production schedule.
(11) Check schedule with suppliers.
(12) Write orders to suppliers.

Design and layout
(1) Copy from writer/obtain client approval.
(2) Cast off copy.
(3) Prepare page layouts.
(4) Order reference prints of photographs/illustrations.
(5) Meeting to discuss layouts.
(6) Write orders to print suppliers, invoices from writer, illustrator, photographer.

Camera-ready artwork
(1) Mark up copy.
(2) Brief typesetter.
(3) Proofread galleys, paste up galleys in position.
(4) Scale photographs, prepare key line artwork, mask and mark photographs.
(5) Flat copy transparency.
(6) Prepare base artwork, plan page imposition.
(7) Check and obtain client approval on artwork.
(8) Prepare print specification, mark up artwork, select printer.
(9) Orders to photographer, typesetter, materials suppliers.

Printing
(1) Assess colour proofs.
(2) Proofs for client approval.
(3) Mark up and return proofs.
(4) Discuss delivery details.
(5) Orders and delivery instructions to printers, invoices from other suppliers.
(6) Cost job and invoice client.

Time involvement on an exhibition stand

Coordinating an exhibition stand is an even more time-consuming activity with comparatively little time spent on design. The designer's task is to see his initial concept through to a finished stand. To do this he must ensure that the activities of many different suppliers dovetail at the right time. The designer has to deal with exhibition contractors, display suppliers and a number of specialists who may be supplying services such as audio-visual programmes or animated displays. It takes careful planning and monitoring as well as comprehensive time and cost recording to maintain a project like this at a profitable level.

On the client side the designer will have a number of contacts – the marketing or publicity manager who is responsible for corporate image; a stand manager who coordinates the company's exhibition programmes, but may not be a communications professional; and product managers who provide specialist advice on particular product displays. The stand would be specially constructed, rather than a prefabricated shell scheme stand, and would feature special graphics, product displays and an audio-visual presentation.

The project might go like this:

Initial briefing
(1) Study organizers' information pack.
(2) Meeting to discuss client requirements.
(3) Set up job file.
(4) Write meeting note/briefing document.

Planning meeting
(1) Meet product/stand managers.
(2) Book stand space.
(3) Agree overall figure for target budget.
(4) Discuss responsibilities.
(5) Draw up list of requirements.
(6) Prepare schedule.
(7) Agree brief for stand.

Initial proposals
(1) Prepare concept visual for stand.
(2) Get first estimate from contractors, organizers.
(3) Prepare working budget.
(4) Report on proposals.
(5) Meeting to discuss proposals, approval to proceed.

Detail design
(1) Discuss display requirements with product managers.
(2) Select photographs.
(3) Plan graphics, captions, product display, audio-visual.
(4) Discuss stand accommodation with stand manager.
(5) Select fittings, carpets, lights from catalogues.
(6) Select unit system or stand fabrication method.
(7) Prepare detail drawings.
(8) Get competitive quotations from contractors.
(9) Cost other elements.
(10) Prepare detail estimates against budget.
(11) Administration – order fittings, services from organizer, graphics from studio, orders to contractors.

Construction
(1) Prepare working drawings and detailed specifications for contractors.
(2) Order prints of graphics, captions.
(3) Order audio-visual equipment and programmes.
(4) Check construction at contractors.
(5) Organize miscellaneous stand materials.

Site work
(1) Organize delivery of all exhibits.
(2) Supervise site construction.

Administration
(1) Agree contractors' suppliers/invoices.
(2) Cost all elements and bill client.

Planning a time-recording system

The principals of monitoring all project time and costs can be applied to any type of design project. The time falls into four main categories – design, client liaison, dealing with suppliers, and project administration – and there are a number of ways of recording it.

Basic time sheets

The traditional method of recording time is by weekly or monthly time sheets which have a horizontal time division and a vertical division to allocate the time against individual project numbers (see Fig. 5.1). The time summaries are transferred to accounts files and the charge for cumulative time is added to other project costs. Time sheets are a familiar method of collecting time, but they have one major drawback. They show cumulative time, but they do not show how that time has been spent, i.e. whether it is management, design, travelling or administration.

This is important information when you come to cost a job, and it is also a useful guide when you are estimating a similar project at a later date. Nor does it distinguish different stages of the project. You might want to make a separate charge for time spent on revised artwork because of author's corrections. If you are invoicing a long project in stages, you have to identify those stages clearly. Submitting an all-costs-to-date figure simply isn't specific enough for you or the client.

Project time sheets

The next stage up is a time sheet that allows more detailed analysis (see Fig. 5.2). It should include charging codes such as design, artwork or management to be allocated against each entry, and should leave room for a minimal description such as redesign, paste up, author's corrections or brief contractor. To fit all that information onto a weekly or monthly time sheet would be difficult; you need a separate time summary for each project. The detail information would normally be transferred from the general time sheet at a convenient time.

Time Summary for the month of _____ June _____ 19 87

Name _____ J an Linton _____

London TYPOGRAPHICAL Designers

Date

Job Nos	1	2	3	4	5	8	9	10	11	12	15	16	17	18	19	22	23	24	25	26	29	30	Totals
6706		2		1								3	1			1					2		10
6707	1			1						4		1	1	2	1								11
6672			3										1		1						2		7
6673			6	5						2	1		1		1								16
6674	3									1	5				1	2							12
6718				1		2										2	1						6
6699		2				2						3				2	1						10
6704						2						3	2				1			1			9
6728	4			5		2		1								1	4			1			18
6729					4		3							2				2					11
6721					4			4									1		4				13
6738							3							2			1		4				10
Tot.hrs	8	2	8	8	8	8	8	6	5	7	6	7	7	8	4	6	3	4	6	8	2	4	

Approved by _____ Date _____

Fig. 5.1 Example of a basic time sheet.

Studio Timesheet

Date	Key	Remarks	BAYES					Totals
15.12.86	A	IDEAS	4½					
16.12.86	A	IDEAS	5½					
17.12.86	A	IDEAS	5½					
18.12.86	A	Rough layouts	6½					
19.12.86	A	" "	2½					
22.12.86	C	Finished mock-up	4½					
23.12.86	C	" "	3½					
24.12.86	C	" "	3					
1 Jan 87	C	" "	3					
2 Jan	C	" "	1					
4 Jan	C	" "	3					
5 Jan	C	" "	4					
8.5.87		HULL – photography	12½					
12.5.87		ILLUSTRATION	3					
27.5.87		TRACES	1½					
28.5.87		MEETING / traces	1 / 1½					

Total hours		
Hourly rate		
Product		

A rough layout
B revised rough layout
C finished layout
D type mark-up
E paste-up
F author's corrections
G artwork
H masking photographs
I administration

Description of artwork produced in LTD studio

Fig. 5.2 Example of a project time sheet.

The importance of monitoring time

Transferring the material from one sheet to another is a mechanical process, and one that is subject to human error. The other drawback of any mechanical recording system is that you never have an up-to-date picture of cumulative costs on a job until completion. It is important to monitor costs on a project to prevent an overspend. Too much time spent on one stage can eat into your estimated allowance and reduce profitability. However, if you are aware of the discrepancies between estimates and costs as they occur, you can either build in compensations at a later stage, or advise your client and budget for additional costs where the work varies from the original brief.

To monitor these costs properly you need to update regularly your costs summaries – a mechanical process that can be very time consuming. The computer has fortunately solved many of the information handling problems, and there are now a number of products on the market that can meet a designer's recording and accounting requirements (see Chapter 3, page 53).

Computer-based recording systems

Computers have information or data handling capabilities far in excess of human capacity. They can transfer data from one file to another, carry out complex calculations, produce reports and forecasts, and store information in the form you want it. That doesn't mean you have to make a substantial capital investment in a large computer installation. A new generation of powerful, easy-to-use personal computers based on microchip technology has made desk-top computing a reality. The computer alone cannot carry out your recording. It needs special software or programs which give the computer the specific set of instructions it needs to carry out those tasks. You can either buy ready-made programs or have one tailor made for your business. General accounting programs for small businesses have been widely available for some time, but now there are ready-made programs specifically developed for businesses like design and architecture, where cost and time recording is a critical element.

One example is a recording and accounting package supplied by Visible Systems Ltd. It has the facilities for traditional time sheet recording and it links those costs to supplier and material costs from other files to computer total costs for individual projects. You can check the records at any time to get an up-to-date picture of cumulative project costs and you can then use the system to create invoices. Additional files on customers show total sales for the period you select, while supplier files show the cumulative and current position on your purchases and the money you owe. The basis of the system is a list of clients; individual project numbers are allocated to the client list and there is a coded list of project activities to help you build up a description. Supplier and employee files allow you to record individual purchases and activities against the project number. You can build in different charging rates for each activity and also compare actual costs with targets. All the data from the various files is merged automatically to give a total project cost and analysis.

As a recording system it has many advantages over mechanical systems. Speed and accuracy of information are the most immediate advantages, but integration with other accounting information can save you time in the long term. You have to keep the information up to date; to do that you make regular entries of information on a conventional keyboard, but because the system performs all the calculations and data transfer, your time involvement is small. A computer can carry out many other tasks in a design business – factors that are discussed in the section on equipment and new technology in Chapter 4 (see page 70), so your decision to buy a particular computing system should not be based on recording and accounting performance alone.

SIX
Expansion

Growth and expansion are key words in the British economy. Every commercial and industrial organization is encouraged to go for growth – according to the politicians it creates wealth and jobs. The expanding economy is a major political objective. But how does this relate to the individual design consultancy and is expansion actually good for everyone?

Expansion doesn't always come in a planned way. Sometimes the sheer volume of work from new and existing clients takes the consultancy beyond its normal capacity. The tell tale signs are a greater number of rush jobs, and more and more overtime. The danger is the false optimism this can raise. Unplanned overload can be variable and short lived. Eye of the Tiger is a design group whose roots were in the record industry designing album covers. At one stage, a major client gave them assignment after assignment, everything wanted in a rush. But, just as suddenly, the flow of work dried up, turnover collapsed and two designers had to laid off.

Planning for expansion is a far more satisfactory solution (see Chapter 1, page 10). In practice, this means looking at the present and future workloads, filling in the gaps where there are any and winning new accounts to build a higher base level. Beresford, for example, now have a four year growth plan with intermediate- and long-term plans to help them at each stage. It is equally important to have a sense of direction. When Crichton broke away from Fitch in 1984 their declared intension was to be in the top ten UK design consultancies in terms of creativity and profitability within five years. Eye of the Tiger have also appointed a marketing and new business manager and now spreads its work among record companies, artists and artists' managers. It is expanding into related areas like magazines, character merchandizing and interiors.

Chapter 2 on marketing discusses in detail the way to develop new business with existing and new clients. Unfortunately, by its very nature, design is a business where short-term solutions and ad hoc projects are the rule rather than the exception. Publicity programmes, for example, are rarely planned in the way that advertising campaigns are. Major packaging projects, new corporate identity programmes, and retail design for large groups have greater elements of continuity, but they usually go to the larger groups who have the current capacity to handle projects of that scale. Clients who have been with a consultancy for a period of time are more cooperative in discussing their plans and timescales. Some might appoint a consultancy for a period of a year with a brief to handle all design work for a specified fee. The norm though is to be given a brief on one project at a time, no real basis for expanding a business. One of the key marketing targets must be clients who can offer opportunities on a large scale and who are prepared to make a long-term commitment to a consultancy that can deliver the goods.

There needs to be a balance between new and existing clients for a number of reasons. Expansion of existing client business indicates good performance, but getting new clients shows the consultancy is outward looking and successful in the marketplace. It is good for staff morale, gives the consultancy a greater client spread and greater protection, and it brings in additional revenue which improves facilities. New business can also benefit existing clients – making better use of resources and improving overall efficiency. It helps the agency develop competitive attitudes, but too much new business too soon can affect the consultancy in other ways, stretching it and having a damaging effect. There are several important signs to look out for. New business should not weaken work for existing clients – they should be kept informed and reassured about new business. New resources and funds should be allocated to new accounts so that the overall standard of service does not fall. Ideally the new business should be in line with the group's overall objectives.

New business development and the stabilization of existing accounts are an essential part of the expansion programme, but so too is the ability to cope with the loss of existing business. There are natural causes for an unplanned reduction in business – costs rising during inflation, products becoming outdated, projects abandoned or marketing personnel changes – all this eats away at planned business levels. So there must be some expansion to stand still. Changes in client contact, competition from other sources, or problems in the quality of work can all contribute to an account loss. If that account makes an important contribution to turnover, it must be replaced. One of the most surprising account changes was Next, moving away from David Davies Associates. The two had seemed an ideal partnership and their joint success was discussed in the press and on television. Yet Davies had already planned to build a broader base – new accounts came in quickly – and he claimed that he had already advised Next to look at other design groups.

Expansion can sometimes take a surprising direction. The natural route for expansion would seem to be in areas of experience, similar markets or similar types of work, but sometimes restrictions on dealing with competitive business can prevent this. How could a consultancy with its base in design of packaging for the food industry expand? Any involvement with design can give the consultancy access to confidential marketing information such as plans for introduction of new products, sales volume and distribution methods. Given that sort of information, it is unlikely that a client would allow a consultancy to work for its competitors. Where can you go if the client does not increase the business he gives the consultancy?

Transferring those skills to non-competitive markets is the natural route. A more unexpected route would be into corporate identity – the skills are related – or possibly into retail design – operating in a similar environment. Coley, Porter, Bell wanted to break out of the packaging mould they believed their clients saw them in; they wanted to use their packaging base to move into corporate identity. The graphic designer specializing in brochures has similar competitive restrictions. The total market for brochures is much larger than the packaging market so this is unlikely to be a serious problem. The brochure designer could also move into company newspapers or magazine design which require similar skills or into editorial design for book publishers.

The consultancy itself can take the initiative and develop new design services to build its business with clients. An interesting development in the retail field is the Piper concept. Set up by former Fitch managing director Crispin Tweddel in 1985, Piper is not strictly speaking a retail design consultancy. It develops business concepts for retail businesses and brings in specialist services like design. But it tackles wider projects like merchandizing, personnel, site presentation and other important aspects of retail. An example was their development of Woolworths' new weekend and leisure store, where they worked with the managing director on the concept and planning, and commissioned Fitch as designers because they understood the problem and the supplier. Piper use this approach to solve problems retail clients bring to them, but they also use it to develop concepts of their own, taking part in joint ventures or developing new products for licensing; they have even opened up a retail outlet of their own. Tweddel believed he had to make the move away from a large consultancy to achieve this. 'At Fitch we talked about merchandising and training,' but he felt that it was difficult to do it credibly from a design base.

Not all moves are related. A consultancy can be asked by its clients to expand its areas of activity – to tackle packaging as well as publication design, or to take on retail design as part of an overall corporate design programme. Here the consultancy is using its knowledge of the client and his market rather than the knowledge of one particular design technique. Eye of the Tiger felt that there was no real barrier to change; as they told *Creative Review*, 'Our whole idea is to create an atmosphere to persuade people to part with their money. The leap from record sleeves to interiors is not too big, we've got plenty of styles in house and we're not afraid to take risks.'

Diversification like this may be part of a consultancy's long-term development strategy to give it a broader base of operations. Such a strategy would be based on a plan for expanding the business over a period of time, say five years. The plan would begin with a statement of where the consultancy saw iteself at the end of that period in terms of business turnover or business profile. Working backwards from that objective it becomes easier to set intermediate targets that build up gradually. Reaching those objectives is not just a matter of hitting financial targets or expanding business; the consultancy may have to change its staffing levels, perhaps look at new premises, look for new sources of finance and consider new methods of organization (see Chapter 1, page 10).

Expansion calls for a strong dose of management; it will not happen by accident. Change should be planned. According to Arthur King & Associates there has to be a ratio between the number of designers and the number of support staff. Larger groups would be at an advantage in dealing with larger clients because they would have a structure that would be able to operate at all different levels. Roberts Weaver, a product design consultancy, believes smaller consultancies grow organically to a certain extent, but to achieve continued growth they would have to appoint someone with full responsibility for sales.

Even a breakaway group like Chrichton – three principals of Fitch who set up in 1984 to break out of the big company mould – believe in expansion by management. They began with an investment of £250,000 and developed a plan that would take them into the top reaches of retail design within five years. They believed that their combined experience of management would get them rapidly through the start-up problems that most new or expanding groups face.

When the business expands, the demands on staff change. For the individual designer, there is the choice of staying single or moving into the unknown territory of partner or employer. The Sheriff-Hugget Partnership, set up in 1985 by two top freelancers, encountered this problem; they felt that they had reached a ceiling in their freelance work – there was only so much work they could do in a day – and there were occasions when their clients needed a higher level of service. Should a small consultancy with, say, three working partners take on another partner or employ others? Larger consultancies already employing a number of designers face a growing problem of delegation and personnel management.

In the early stages of expansion, it may be sufficient to work longer hours and rely on overtime to cope with the higher level of work. This is rarely a satisfactory solution because jobs become rushed with little time for real consideration. An alternative is to take on freelancers while the workload is building up. Freelance services do not add to the overheads and are a flexible form of support while conditions are changing. The problem is that you have less control over freelance staff, they may have other commitments and they may not be familiar enough with the work to cope with a rush job. The question is knowing what stage to take on permanent staff. It comes when there is sufficient work to keep existing staff fully occupied with enough work for one more designer. Whether the new recruits should be specialists or have adaptable skills depends on the long-term plan. If the consultancy is expanding into unfamiliar territory, a specialist can take on the new work with the minimum of retraining. But if there no such definite direction someone who is able to take on a variety of work would be a better choice.

As the number of staff grows it becomes more difficult to control the flow of work through a studio. The number of jobs and their complexity make forward planning and control an important management task. The question of delegation is discussed more fully in the section on staff in Chapter 4 (see page 68). Allied to this is the question of productivity and profitability – extra staff add to the company's overheads. The decision to recruit is taken when the workload is at a critical level, so to maintain productivity and profit it is important that the workload is increased. Productivity is measured as the level of work that each employee is handling. Assuming that the designers work at a similar rate, their level of productivity will depend directly on the amount of work they have to handle (see Chapter 4, page 68).

Finance is another important consideration in an expanding business. An expansion programme makes new demands on a company's financial structure – a higher level of working capital to cover the cost of larger premises, more employees, more sophisticated equipment and increased payments to suppliers. The extra money required would be partially financed out of the higher level of income from increased turnover, but this depends on prompt payment by clients. Good credit control and cash flow management is therefore an important part of expansion funding (see Chapter 3, page 50).

A growing number of design groups are going public to raise additional funds. Shares in the consultancy, which were formally held by the directors and a limited number of private shareholders, are offered for sale to the public. When the shares have been sold the public is effectively the owner of the company and the directors are responsible to their public shareholders. The proceeds of the sale of the shares provides the company with its additional source of finance. At the time of publication a number of designers have gone public – Aidcom International, Michael Peters, WPP, Craton Knight Lodge, Holmes and Marchant, Fitch and McColl – and there were others in related industries – Saatchi, Howard Spink, Addison Page Communications. Although it is a comparatively recent phenomenon this is likely to be a growing trend among communications consultancies.

There are a number of routes for going public. Getting a full listing means becoming a full member of the Stock Exchange – a status that is unlikely to apply to most design groups because of their relatively small size. However, the Unlisted Securities Market (USM) has been set up recently to help smaller organizations go public. The larger firms of accountants publish guides to going public which give outline and detailed information on the routes to follow. They suggest that you need a considerable amount of professional advice from accountants, solicitors and other advisers to meet with the regulations and achieve a successful flotation. Retail analyst John Richards has been deeply involved with the movement of design groups onto the USM. At stockbrokers Capel Cure Myers he was responsible for setting up *Retail* magazine which focused attention on the effect designers were having on the retail market. He also analysed the successes of creative services on the USM and helped to bring design groups to the notice of investors.

A consultancy planning to go public has to prepare a full set of accounts and a prospectus which gives investors detailed information on their activities and performance. Most design consultancies would be able to cope with the production of the prospectus themselves; stockbrokers and analysts can give advice on the contents and emphasis in the prospectus. When The Media Department went public, stockbrokers Philips and Drew put together a proposal document for them. Its contents included:

- Directors and advisers
- Summary of information – business track record, placing statistics

- History of the company – founders and growth
- Development of specialist media companies – context of the business
- Success of media specialists – why they are used
- TMD's success
- Main services
- Operational structure
- Clients
- TMD's market position
- Profit and financial information
- Prospects
- Accountant's report and financial information.

Going public gives consultancies access to funds for expansion. Their ability to raise additional finance is related to the share price and their overall performance. This is seen as the price at which investors are prepared to buy or sell their shares. The better the performance, the higher the share price because more people will want to follow a successful company. The workings of the Stock Market are in practice more complex and subtle than that but the reality is that the design group is now judged on its financial performance as much as its design activities. The business emphasis now becomes very different, as Michael Peters found out. He found that he had to keep diversifying and showing a profit that would please the City; his very successful packaging business would not prove a wide enough base for real growth. The speed of growth too was difficult – the City wanted fast growth whereas the consultancy felt gradual slow growth would prove more of an advantage in the long term.

A high profile becomes an essential part of the practice's operations. Here the advice of a public relations consultancy specializing in the financial relations can be valuable. Their task is to ensure that the financial community, particularly investors and their advisers, are fully aware of your activities and can base their assessment on an understanding of your organization. The annual report gives designers the opportunity to demonstrate their professionalism as well as their corporate performance (see Chapter 2, page 25).

Also under scrutiny is the way the practice develops and the way it expands its activities. Going public provides the capital for expansion but investors are looking to see whether their investment is being spent wisely. They look for sound management and an indication that the business is stable and growing. How much do analysts know about design groups – do they know what contributes to success? Some believe in diversification or international expansion, but this may take a group far from its origins. Management performance and the structure of the company therefore becomes important. The problem is to behave creatively and profitably. Wolff Olins discussed the dilemma. The Stock Market is not about appealing to designers and clients, but appealing to investors and analysts whose attitude may be 'Never mind the quality, are the profits there?' Other people question whether creativity can be managed and whether it can survive the financial and organizational changes that are needed in a public company.

Expansion means that greater attention should be paid to marketing and financial management. Now they might need the attention of a specialist manager, perhaps recruiting people from outside to fill the gaps in internal management. In preparation for a possible flotation on the USM, Wolff Olins appointed a second managing director to partner Brian Boylan who had sixteen years' experience in the company. The new managing director helped to set up business systems and structures that were essential to the growth of the consultancy. When he left, Boylan became sole managing director once again, but the consultancy was quick to appoint a new finance director to complement Boyland's own abilities. Conran had Arlene Gould, a London Business School graduate of Design Management who was responsible for the group's long-term business strategy (see Chapter 4, page 67).

The changes may be more fundamental than just management changes – they may involve restructuring the company. When the Michael Peters Group went public they set up a number of new subsidiary companies to handle specialist aspects of design – the Annual Report Group, Creative Concepts, and Right Angle Design for example – companies with separate names but working under the Michael Peters banner. Aidcom set up a company called Concept Development International to generate new product ideas and product ranges for major retailers. Wolff Olins set up satellite companies operating under the Wolff Olins banner, the first was Wolff Olins Interiors, but the planned list included public relations, corporate advertising and perhaps product development – all of them related to their core business with a bias towards communications. These were set up initially as extra services for clients already working with Wolff Olins on corporate identity; they were building on existing strengths rather than moving into new areas.

Within the consultancy, it is possible to develop staff skills around a particular market area – individuals or small groups who specialize in retail or packaging, computer business or consumer products. By building up specialist experience in individual staff, smaller consultancies can emulate the major developments of their larger rivals.

The kind of expansion we have described so far takes place by reorganization or by adding to the consultancy's resources. An alternative is the merger or takeover route. Here the consultancy goes into partnership with another consultancy or buys it out and takes over ownership. This kind of association can be valuable if the other consultancy is already established in the markets you are aiming at, or if it has a client base which is compatible with your own. Beresford and Partners chose the merger route. They established an association with a company in interiors and graphics so that they could offer their clients an integrated service. They had no plans to become a major group but they felt that multidisciplinary skills would enable them to compete effectivly.

Sutherland Haws merged with a communications consultancy, giving them a broader client base and access to other services for clients who want more than design; they are also expanding their retail and interiors section. Design group SMS and market research company Axiom cooperated on a research study into design in the health market; the designers were keen to get more involved in marketing, and they felt that the research project they had worked on gave them greater credibility when they were talking to clients. Holmes and Marchant, a design and sales promotion company, set up a subsidiary, Financial Statements, and was investigating a new product development division. Brand Action was a company set up after Bamber Forsyth Design merged with advertising agency Cromer Titterton Mills Cowday. The company was to provide new product development services together with retail and marketing. These mergers gave the designers additional services which they could draw on in a competitive situation (see Chapter 2, page 23).

Such mergers can allow designers to continue running their own business but give them better access to funds and support services. A number of other mergers between advertising agencies and design groups took place in the mid 1980s. One of the most ambitious of these communications groups was the WPP group, set up by former Saatchi and Saatchi finance director, Martin Sorrell. His aim was to establish a multinational below-the-line marketing services company. Already he had acquired companies in sales promotion, video, design and incentive marketing. The design acquisitions included Oakley Young Associates and Sampson Tyrell. Sorrell's offer to the designers was to provide financial management services to complement their specialist skills; that, he believed, was one of their weak points. To help the companies reach their full potential he set them ambitious but realistic growth targets of twenty per cent – well within the forty per cent growth rate he had analysed for the design business. Although design itself had become acceptable as a powerful marketing tool, he believed that the industry was still fragmented and that multinational clients needed evidence of sound management. His aim was to bring that sort of discipline to the business and to provide a wide range of professional marketing services to the multinationals.

There are many other reasons for a merger and they can be built into a formal grid of merger options. Mergers give ready-made growth and are a means of rapid expansion, but like other ready-made solutions there is no guarantee that they will work or that the partners will be compatible. The wrong people, clients who object to the new arrangements, confusion over responsibilities and information that was not revealed before the merger, people who fear that the next stage could be rationalization – these are all possible problems with a merger, but if it works then both parties benefit.

Expansion is not limited to specific markets; geographical expansion on a regional or international scale is a strategy that is already widely practised by the advertising business – but little by designers. In advertising there is a very strong distinction between London and regional offices in important centres like Manchester, Leeds or Scotland which give a local service to larger clients. To some clients they may simply be providing local support to a national account, but to others they offer a national service at a local level. No such regionalization seems to affect the design industry, although clients do make an artificial distinction between London and provincial design groups.

Is regional expansion a practical proposition? Look at your client list to see the geographical spread and see how easy it is to service those accounts from your present location. In practice many can be handled remotely with a combination of regular visits and telephone discussion. If the volume of work from one remote client and the level of travelling rose to a very high level it would prove more efficient to handle it from a local office. You then have to assess whether that local office could form the basis of a successful business in its own right. Is there an opportunity for other business in the same area? The new local consultancy has few of the advantages of the parent company. Unless a large number of staff transfer to the new location, there are few central resources that a design group can draw on to achieve economies of scale. It is essentially a new design group.

One experiment that could benefit from the development of new technology is the growth of instant art studios – similar in concept to the chains of instant print shops. They are not full service studios in the strict sense because they handle a limited range of work and concentrate naturally on the high volume end of the market – producing straightforward sales and technical leaflets quickly and economically. Their main investment seems to be in equipment that can speed up production – in-house typesetting, page make-up terminals, electronic retouching equipment and computer graphics terminals.

Local branches are often set up on a franchise basis so that the manager is effectively a self-employed person who is supplied with a standard range of equipment, and supported by national or regional brand advertising. The customer is offered a standard product at a fixed price with a firm indication of delivery. In many cases, the studios are tied to an instant print shop so that the customer gets a complete package from layout to printed job.

One ambitious project involved an American company called Qwikcolor; they had built up a successful operation in the USA offering unheard of delivery times on standard A4 four-page colour leaflets designed and printed in just four hours. Their service was built around a range of high technology equipment covering every production stage, so that they could handle the whole operation in-house. Unfortunately, what they were unable to do in the UK was convince the financial community of their case and they failed to raise enough money for more than one outlet. Nevertheless, they showed the way ahead, and the presence of that type of operation could threaten a considerable proportion of bread-and-butter studio work.

Expansion on an international scale can stretch the consultancy's resources even further. The advertising agency business is showing increasing signs of operating on a global scale. For over twenty-five years there has been a multinational aspect to the agency business – dominated in the main by American groups. In the mid 1980s global agency operations are increasing and one of the factors behind this is the growth in global marketing by their clients. Clients want the same level of service in every country. Why then should this not apply to the design business in a field like packaging or corporate identity? The Belgian group, Design Board, had the multinational Procter and Gamble Group as one of their main clients; they were responsible for designing all the packaging that was used internationally.

Similar problems of expansion apply at international level; a design consultancy is a collection of individuals, and there are few transferrable talents or resources. Yet, this has not stopped a number of British design groups from becoming successful exporters.

The Design Network has been exploiting modern technology and communications to build international markets. They are part of a group of associated studios currently based in London, Milan, Brussels, Switzerland and the USA. The studios have compatible graphics equipment and use communications systems to send material from one location to another. If there is an overload they can transfer work, or if they have a specialist project it can be handled by the right person. Pentagram first established business in the USA in 1978 to provide a local service for their European clients. More recently they have set up an office in California to deal with new opportunities in the Far East. They have not done this by exporting Pentagram staff; instead, they have set up an association with local consultancies who share their philosophy and standards. Michael Peters believes it is also important to have an American base – travelling designers do not provide the level of service the clients needs. He has worked with American clients on a number of different projects – particularly in the packaging field – but feels that in the long term he will be more successful in exporting high technology design.

The practical problem is one of travelling and handling projects at arms length. Cope with that and you can handle international business. There are other ways of handling international accounts that don't involve direct contact. You could deal with associate companies who are effectively providing a marketing service for you. They represent you in local markets and handle administration and liaison while passing work on to you; this is a simple method of marketing but it does give you less control over the work and the way you handle it.

Overseas expansion doesn't always turn out to be successful. In 1985 Fitch announced that it was closing a number of its overseas offices – it had offices in Paris, Milan and the Middle East – arguing that it needed local people to understand and coordinate local projects, especially if they were complex. The high overheads and general rising costs eventually made this an uneconomic proposition, and they ran their overseas business from London. Aidcom agreed that the high set-up and running costs of maintaining a local office – as they did in Paris and Singapore – could be prohibitively expensive and this discouraged them from even thinking about a start-up in certain parts of the world. When they decided to set up in the USA, they bought the services of a San Francisco design group rather than import staff and skills across the Altantic. As the business develops, the plan is to exchange staff and know-how.

The point of expansion is to grow in size, to handle larger and more complex projects or simply to increase turnover and profit. It begs the question whether designers want to work in a large organization and whether clients feel they need the services of a large organization. While the large consultancies are growing larger, there are an increasing number of breakaways.

Fitch and Company is one of the largest consultancies; only organizations of such size, they argue, have the resources to tackle projects like the redesign of giant store groups. In 1984, a number of Fitch principals left to set up their own businesses. Part of their reason was the sheer size of the organization, yet their declared intention was to set up a large successful consultancy within five years. Perhaps it is the challenge of growth rather than size itself that is the incentive. Eye of the Tiger found that, when they advertised for designers, many of the applications came from designers already with large consultancies; they were looking for the challenge of smaller organizations. They felt that design at the top of the league was full of superbly run businesses, but was creatively stagnant. It was a common belief that smaller consultancies were more aggressive – larger consultancies offered safe solutions. A more restrained view was that the larger and smaller consultancies could live comfortably together.

Large clients needed the service and people of a similar organization while smaller clients felt that they would get more recognition and attention in a smaller design group. Several of the larger consultancies recognized the potentially impersonal nature of their organizations; to overcome that, they were restructuring the company as a series of departments so that the client could work with a small team and get a degree of continuity in working relationships. Locke Peterson aims to grow into a strong multidisciplinary consultancy; they believe the pressure will be on smaller groups to retain business as the larger public practices expand relentlessly. On the advice of a management consultant, they have identified seven areas where they could grow profitably. The danger they recognize is that, in growing large, they could lose the element of personal contact that is so important. The solution is to set up a series of separate divisions, breaking down the company into a series of small units so that growth and size can be controlled.

Smaller consultancies offer a more personal service, but they are prone to sudden changes in personnel – a factor which can have a dramatic effect on client/consultancy relationships. Larger consultancies can afford to be more flexible in their staff arrangements, they can provide back-up and a level of service that smaller organizations could not match, and they have the financial resources to ensure long-term stability.

One of the very real problems of expansion is the danger of a gap growing between design and management. Wolff Olins admits there is a risk that management could demand work that is predictable. Wally Olins himself, though not a designer, spent most of his time in representing the company to clients and working on special projects. Conran Associates is a very successful consultancy, but the price of success was that the profit became more important than design. Many top people left, others only came to get the Conran name on their CV. In 1984 they lost a quarter of their designers, lost their sharp edge and were going backwards in design terms. The in-house team was booming because of all the design work for the Storehouse group, yet Conran Design was suffering.

Reasons for expansion

The following sections look at the reasons why design groups expand. Expansion is not always planned and designers have to cope with overload as well as a smooth transition to a larger size. For those who want to expand their business, there is a wide range of options and these sections show the possibilities in each.

Coping with overload

For many designers, expansion begins with an increasing workload. Existing clients ask for urgent delivery of a high volume of work, they keep on briefing one large project after another, or new clients come in bringing additional work. If the workload has been low up to that point this could be beneficial; it means that the number of chargeable hours will increase, making more efficient use of staff time. But if the staff are already fully occupied this raises a problem. The first move is to work overtime, but there are physical limits to the amount of overtime that can be worked without affecting the quality and accuracy of work. Staff have other commitments in their own time, and an excessive amount of continuous overtime can affect morale. The decision is whether to take on additional staff or bring in freelance support (see Chapter 4, page 66).

Much depends on the ability to forecast the duration of the high level of work. If it is only a short-term boom, you should cope as best you can, using freelance support on work that can be put out and keeping your own staff on projects that need detailed attention. But if the workload remains at that high level, additional permanent staff are essential. The problem is to recruit effective people quickly.

You have to allow time for advertising, selection and a period of notice. Even when a new designer begins, there is still an initial settling in period before he becomes fully effective.

New business from clients

It is far more satisfactory when clients plan their requirements in advance and give you a programme for a period of a year. Unfortunately, given the ad hoc nature of most design projects it is difficult to make long-term forecasts. When the future workload is established, you can plan staffing levels – a major retail project with a set completion date, for example, is going to need a certain number of designers for a specific period of time.

Planned expansion

Planned expansion takes the element of risk out of expansion and puts it firmly under your control. Here you are not coping with overload or responding to the demands of clients but you set the target for growth and allocate your resources according to the targets. Planned expansion is based on a series of long-term and intermediate targets which cover business levels, marketing programmes, staffing and financial requirements.

Setting objectives for expansion

Planned expansion needs a specific direction. It is not enough to say you want to grow bigger. How much do you want to grow by? Where do you want to end up? Objectives, as we discussed in an earlier section, can take many forms. You may want to become the largest UK design consultancy, but this has to be put in specific terms; to reach that position may require growth of thirty per cent per annum for four years. Your objectives should cover the position you want to reach, the timescale for reaching intermediate targets, and it should cover the resources that are needed (see Chapter 1, page 10).

Growth from existing clients

This is perhaps the easiest form of business development, although you should not take your position for granted. One barrier to growth with your own clients is that they often make assumptions about their suppliers – that they only provide a specific type of service and do not move outside their speciality, and that they do not have unlimited capacity. It is important to let clients know the full range of services you supply. You can also develop new services for your clients. To do this you need to carry out an audit of the client's business, looking at areas where different types of design service would be useful, and seeing how these services are currently supplied. New business from existing clients offers less risk in purchasing terms to the client. They are already aware of the level of service you offer and they know that you can perform.

Existing services to new clients

Here the design group is opening up new markets for its existing services; it may have already reached saturation point with existing clients. The skill is to identify prospects with requirements for similar services. It is difficult to deal with prospects in the same market; clients are not keen on suppliers who deal with their competitors. How serious a barrier this is depends on the confidentiality of the work.

New types of business

The most difficult type of expansion is the introduction of new product or new services – services that you are not currently offering your clients or prospects. There may be a need for the service because no one is currently supplying it, or because you recognize a need for an entirely new service. Chapter 2 on marketing shows how to develop new products.

This new service may require skills that are not currently available in the consultancy. Chapter 4 on personnel management shows that this may involve a need for new recruitment and training to get staff of the right calibre. It may also require investment in new equipment.

New types of business carry the greatest level of risk. The clients are unknown and you are working to different standards.

Regional and national growth

Geography has rarely been a problem for the design consultancy. Although there is a traditional bias towards London design groups, this does not change the basic problem of location. Regional designers have claimed their services are every bit as good as the London studios and there is little evidence to dispute that. Many regional groups have set up local offices taking fast delivery services and communications to keep material moving. A sales office may be all that is needed to service the customer.

There has been a move at the lower end of the scale to set up regional chains of artwork studios; these are run on a franchise basis on the lines of instant print shops, but they only offer a limited quality service. The difficulty for anyone wishing to set up a network of full service studios is to maintain the right level of staff. The solution may be to set up a central office where the work can be done and to use the local offices as service centres.

Geographical expansion is a useful option if the service you are offering is a specialist one and your clients are in scattered locations. The main problem is one of time, time spent travelling to meetings which is non-productive time. If the service you are offering is based on rapid turnround then regional work could be a problem.

Mergers and takeovers

Design is a profession that has traditionally developed along the lines of private practice – individual designers or independent consultancies. As the earlier sections of theis chapter showed, expansion can depend on new skills or access to new markets. To achieve this through natural growth and development could take a long time and the marketing opportunity will be lost. Mergers and takeovers can provide a shortcut. A strategic link can quickly put a growing practice into a more competitive position.

A merger can work in both directions. You may take the initiative because you have recognized specific weaknesses or opportunities that a merger can overcome. Even a situation where you are the unexpected target for a merger or takeover can work in your favour if it stabilizes the business or gives you new marketing opportunities. As the rest of his section shows, there is no automatic benefit from a merger; change has to be carefully managed – particularly in the post-merger period – to get the real benefit.

Assessing the merger

A merger must have practical benefits for both sides, but, for the company initiating the move, there must be positive benefits. A checklist for a merger might include the following points:

- What are the company's strengths and weaknesses in its main markets?
- What sort of market penetration does it have?
- What would it add to your current performance in the market?
- What will the move cost, and is there a more cost-effective way of achieving the same objective?
- What long-term potential do they have?
- What alternatives are there to a merger?

You should also assess the quality of the people you will be working with. What sort of performance have they turned in recently? Is their management stable? And, most important, would you be able to work with them? A merger is both a marketing decision and a personal decision.

Arranging the merger

A merger is a financially based deal; whether it is a merger or a takeover depends on the type and level of payment and whether there is one dominant partner. It can be an outright purchase in which the initiator pays cash or some other form of remuneration for the other company, or it can involve share exchanges, in which shares of different values are exchanged or given to the other company. The principles behind share deals are complex and beyond the scope of this book. Any deal should be based on a formal agreement between the two companies, covering their future responsibilities and the allocation of resources and profits. These legal agreements should be separate from any informal agreements over working practices.

You should take advice from accountants and solicitors (see Chapter 3, page 62).

Working together

A merger is a working arrangement between two parties to improve their joint performance. In practical terms, this means finding the best way to benefit from the joint resources. At board meetings, for example, directors from both companies would take joint responsibility for policy decisions, although day-to-day decisions might remain with individuals. However, if the merger leads to radical changes in working arrangements, where some staff find themselves demoted or even redundant, this could cause problems. Client conflict is another potential problem area, which has been highlighted by the large number of global mergers among advertising agencies. Generally, clients find it unacceptable to have their suppliers working for competitors, but this depends on the type of design work that is being handled. The combined strength of the two consultancies should create an opportunity to expand the business, making conflict less of a problem.

Multidisciplinary groups

An increasing number of mergers are taking place to build communications groups. The instigator could be an advertising agency and the other members might include a public relations consultancy, marketing company, research bureau, sales promotion consultancy, and a number of specialist design groups. This grouping gives the individual members access to the resources of all the other group members so that they can tackle larger and more complex projects that need a variety of skills. They also get access to group financial resources to fund expansion or allow them to take on large long-term projects that could present cash flow problems to a small consultancy. The individual companies can either continue to trade under their own names, or take on a group corporate identity. Much depends on the value of their established name and their relationship with clients.

References

Chapter 1 Business Matters

Information on management training

British Institute of Management   Management House, Cottingham Road, CORBY, Northants NN17 1TT

Chartered Society of Designers   12 Carlton House Terrace, LONDON SW1Y 5AH

Design Business Group   12 Carlton House Terrace, LONDON SW1Y 5AH

Design Council   28 Haymarket, LONDON SW1Y 4SU

London Business School   Sussex Place, Regents Park, LONDON NW1

London Enterprise Agency   4 Snowhill, LONDON EC1

Information on design

Chartered Society of Designers   12 Carlton House Terrace, LONDON SW1Y 5AH

Design Business Group   12 Carlton House Terrace, LONDON SW1Y 5AH

Design Week survey of consultancies   *Design Week*, Centaur Communications Limited, St Giles House, 50 Poland Street, LONDON W1V 4AX

Design Week survey of public companies *Design Week*, Centaur Communications Limited, St Giles House, 50 Poland Street, LONDON W1V 4AX

Magazines on design

Blueprint   26 Cramer Street, LONDON W1M 3HE

Campaign   Marketing Publications Limited, 30 Lancaster Gate, LONDON W2 3LY

Creative Review   Centaur Communications Limited, St Giles House, 50 Poland Street, LONDON W1V 4AX

Design   Design Council, 28 Haymarket, LONDON SW1Y 4SU

Design Week   Centaur Communications Limited, St Giles House, 50 Poland Street, LONDON W1V 4AX

Designers Journal   Architectural Press Limited, 9 Queen Anne's Gate, LONDON SW1H 9BY

Direction   Marketing Publications Limited, 30 Lancaster Gate, LONDON W2 3LY

The Financial Times

Graphics World   Graphics World Publications, 7 Brewer Street, MAID-STONE, Kent ME14 1RU

Marketing   Marketing Publications Limited, 30 Lancaster Gate, LONDON W2 3LY

Marketing Week   Centaur Communications Limited, St Giles House, 50 Poland Street, LONDON W1V 4AX

Books

Goslett, Dorothy (1978) *Professional Practice of Design*. Batsford.

Lorenz, Christopher, *The Design Dimension*. Oxford: Basil Blackwell.

Pentagram Design Partnership (1978) *Living by Design*. Lund Humphries.

Chapter 2   Marketing

Professional advisers

Advertising Association   Abford House, 15 Wilton Road, LONDON SW1V 1NJ

Association of Conference Executives   Riverside House, High Street, HUNTINGDON, Cambs PE18 6SG

Institute of Marketing   Moor Hall, Cookham, MADENHEAD, Berks SL6 9QH

Institute of Public Relations   Gate House, St John's Square, LONDON EC1M 4DH

Institute of Practitioners in Advertising   44 Belgrave Square, LONDON SW1X 8QS

Market Research Society   175 Oxford Street, LONDON W1R 1TA

Public Relations Consultants Association   10 Belgrave Square, LONDON SW1X 8PH

Directories

Advertisers' Annual   British Media Publications, Windsor Court, East Grinstead House, EAST GRINSTEAD, West Sussex RH19 1XA

British Rate and Data   76 Oxford Street, LONDON W1N 9FD

Creative Handbook   British Media Publications, Windsor Court, East Grinstead House, EAST GRINSTEAD, West Sussex RH19 1XA

Exhibition Bulletin   The London Bureau, 266–272 Kirkdale, Sydenham, LONDON SE26 4RZ

London Creative Listings   Kogan Page Limited, 120 Pentonville Road, LONDON N1 9JN

Magazines

Campaign   Marketing   Publications   Limited,   30   Lancaster   Gate, LONDON W2 3LY

Conference World Association of Conference Executives, Riverside House, High Street, HUNTINGDON, Cambs PE18 6SG
Creative Review Centaur Communications Limited, St Giles House, 50 Poland Street, LONDON W1V 4AX
Design Week Centaur Communications Limited, St Giles House, 50 Poland Street, LONDON W1V 4AX
Graphics World Graphics World Publications, 7 Brewer Street, MAIDSTONE, Kent ME14 1RU
Industrial Marketing Digest Frederick Polhill Limited, The Old Rectory, Ranmore Common, DORKING, Surrey RH5 6SP
Marketing Marketing Publications Limited, 30 Lancaster Gate, LONDON W2 3LY
Marketing Week Centaur Communications Limited, St Giles House, 50 Poland Street, LONDON W1V 4AX
Media Week Media Week Limited, 20–22 Wellington Street, LONDON WC2E 7DD
What's New in Marketing Morgan Grampian Limited, Morgan Grampian House, Calderwood Street, LONDON SE18 6QH

Books

Andrews, Les (ed.) (1984) *The Post Office Direct Mail Handbook*. Exley.
Brackman, Henrietta (1984), The Perfect Portfolio. Columbus Books.
Cannon, Tom (1980) *Basic Marketing*. Holt, Rinehart & Winston.
Cannon, Tom & Willis, Mike (19) *How to Buy and Sell Overseas*. Business Books.
Davidson, Hugh, *Offensive Marketing*.
Davis, Martyn (1981) *The Effective Use of Advertising Media*. Business Books.
Fairlie, Robin (1979) *Direct Mail*. Kogan Page.
Farbey, David (1979) *The Business of Advertising*. Associated Business Press.
Fletcher, Winston (1983) *Meetings, Meetings, Meetings*. Michael Joseph.
Golzen, Godfrey, Colin Barrow, and Jackie Severn (1985) *Taking up a Franchise*. Kogan Page.
Hibert, F.P., *The Principles and Practice of Marketing Export*. Heinemann.
Linton, Ian, *Promotion for the Professions*. Kogan Page.
Mendelsohn, Martin (1984) *The Guide to Franchising*. Pergamon Press.
Turner, Stuart, *Thorson's Guide to Making Business Presentations*. Thorson.
Wilson, Aubrey, *Marketing Professional Services*.
Wilson, Aubrey (1984) *Practical Development for Professionals*. McGraw-Hiu.

Design information services

BBC Design Award Scheme Design Council, 28 Haymarket, LONDON SW1Y 4SU
Design Week Leads *Design Week*, Centaur Communications Limited, St

Giles House, 50 Poland Street, LONDON W1V 4AX
Designer Selection Service Design Council, 28 Haymarket, LONDON SW1Y 4SU
Support for Design Design Council, 28 Haymarket, LONDON SW1Y 4SU

Chapter 3   Financial Management

Professional advisers

Chartered Institute of Management Accountants 63 Portland Place, LONDON W1N 4AP
Institute of Chartered Accountants in England & Wales Chartered Accountants Hall, Moorgate Place, LONDON EC2P 2BJ
Law Society 113 Chancery Lane, LONDON WC2A 1PL

Books

Barrow, Colin (1984) *Financial Management for the Small Business*. Kogan Page.
Simons, Leon (1983) *The Basic Arts of Financial Management*. Business Books.
Touche Roses & Co., *Tolley's Survival Kit for Small Businesses*. Tolley Publishing.

Magazines

Financial Decisions VNU Business Publications Limited, 32–34 Broadwick Street, LONDON W1A 2HG
Management Today Management Publications Limited, 30 Lancaster Gate, LONDON W2 3LY
Mind Your Own Business 106 Church Street, LONDON SE19 2UB

Chapter 4   Personnel Management

Professional advisers

Chartered Society of Designers 12 Carlton House Terrace, LONDON SW1Y 5AH
Design Business Group 12 Carlton House Terrace, LONDON SW1Y 5AH
Design and Industries Association 17 Lawn Crescent, KEW GARDENS, Surrey TW9 3NR
Institute of Personnel Management IPM House, Camp Road, LONDON SW19 4UW

Education and training

CAM Foundation Abford House, 15 Wilton Road, LONDON SW1V 1NJ
National Computing Centre Oxford Road, MANCHESTER M1 7ED

Books

Goslett, Dorothy (1978) *The Professional Practice of Design*. Batsford.
Thomason, George (1981) *A Textbook of Personnel Management*. IPM.
Allsopp, Michael (1979) *Management in the Professions*. Business Books.

Magazines

Business Systems and Equipment McLean Hunter Limited, 76 Oxford Street, LONDON W1N 9FD
Design Week Centaur Communications Limited, St Giles House, 50 Poland Street, LONDON W1V 4AX
Graphics World Graphics World Publications, 7 Brewer Street, MAIDSTONE, Kent ME14 1RU
Mind Your Own Business 106 Church Street, LONDON SE19 2UB

Chapter 5   Project Management

Suppliers trade associations

Association of Exhibition Contractors 9 Totteridge Avenue, HIGH WYCOMBE, Bucks HP13 6XG
Association of Illustrators 1 Colville Place, LONDON W1P 1HN
British Contract Furnishing Association PO Box 384, LONDON N12 8HF
British Exhibition Contractors Association Kingsmere House, Graham Road, LONDON SW19 3SR
British Institute of Professional Photography 2 Amwell End, WARE, Herts SG12 9HN
British Printing Industries Federation 11 Bedford Row, LONDON WC1R 4DX
Market Research Society 175 Oxford Street, LONDON W1R 1TA

Magazines

Audio Visual
Blueprint 26 Cramer Street, LONDON W1M 3HE
British Journal of Photography Henry Greenwood & Co., 28 Great James Street, LONDON WC1N 3HL
Design Design Council, 28 Haymarket, LONDON SW1Y 4SU
Design Week Centaur Communications Limited, St Giles House, 50 Poland Street, LONDON W1V 4AX
Designers Journal Architectural Press Limited, 9 Queen Anne's Gate, LONDON SW1H 9BY
Graphics World Graphics World Publications, 7 Brewer Street, MAIDSTONE, Kent ME14 1RU
Lighting & Design McLean Hunter Limited, 76 Oxford Street, LONDON W1N 9FD
Professional Photographer Mclaren Publishers, PO Box 109, Mclaren House, Scarbrook Road, CROYDON, Surrey CR9 1QH

RIBA Interiors   RIBA Magazines Limited, 66 Portland Place, LONDON W1N 4AD

What's New in Interiors   Morgan Grampian Limited, Morgan Grampian House, Calderwood Street, LONDON SE18 6QH

Directories

Creative Handbook   British Media Publications, Windsor Court, East Grinstead House, EAST GRINSTEAD, West Sussex RH19 1XA

Writer's and Artist's Yearbook   A & C Black.

Chapter 6   Expansion

Most of the references given for the preceding chapters will be useful.

Index

Structure of design 14, 15
Suppliers 87
Support for Design 13, 26, 42
Sutherland Haws 100

Taxation 42, 44, 59–61

Technology and design 11, 70–4, 102
Tesco 6
The Media Department 98, 99
Timesheets 53, 54, 89–92
Training 12, 67
Typesetters 82

Value Added Tax 60
Visible Systems 92

WCRS 16
W. H. Smith 6, 23, 75
Willings Press Guide 33
Wolff Olins 7, 8, 16, 24, 99, 100, 104
Woolworth 96
Word processing 72, 83
WPP 6, 98, 101
Writers 83, 84

Emma Jane Began

73, Fantygary Rd

CF6 9DT